TUXEDOS TO TAILGATES

A Celebration

of the Seasons

ꝏ

Recipes & Menus
from the Dallas Junior Forum

DALLAS JUNIOR FORUM

Founded in 1977, Dallas Junior Forum is one of nine chapters of Junior Forums, Inc., a Texas-based service organization. Our mission is to create a greater interest among women in civic, educational, and philanthropic endeavors by serving the community through volunteer work.

The members of Dallas Junior Forum are dedicated to improving our community through both direct service and by providing grants to worthwhile charitable projects. Our efforts focus primarily on children, women, and the elderly.

In 1986, the women of Dallas Junior Forum created *Deep In The Heart*, a best-selling cookbook that won the prestigious Tabasco Hall of Fame award in 2000.

Proceeds from the sale of *Tuxedos to Tailgates* will support the charities of Dallas Junior Forum.

TUXEDOS TO TAILGATES

A Celebration of the Seasons

Recipes & Menus from the Dallas Junior Forum

Published by Dallas Junior Forum.

Design and Art Direction: Pamela Glick Creative

This cookbook is a collection of favorite recipes, which are not necessarily original recipes.

Library of Congress Control Number: 2002111218
ISBN: 0-9617187-1-4

Edited and Manufactured by
Favorite Recipes® Press
An imprint of

FRP

Manufactured in the United States of America
First Printing 2003
15,000 copies

TUXEDOS TO TAILGATES

A Celebration

of the Seasons

Recipes & Menus
from the Dallas Junior Forum

Contents

෨෨

Spring 7

Summer 51

PREFACE

❧

Entertaining. The word brings to mind the laughter, stories, and precious memories created whenever family, friends, and food come together. It is a time to celebrate and a time that will draw you closer. Entertaining means a special dinner for your family, a casual event for friends, or a formal affair with colleagues—and anything in between.

Tuxedos to Tailgates is a book of seasonal entertaining: seasonal to capture the feel and style of the moment, entertaining because there is always a reason to gather together with those you love.

The women of Dallas Junior Forum bring you a collection of recipes that express the joy and love that goes into the meals we prepare when we are entertaining. We combined delicious dishes and seasonal fare with charming and distinctive themes.

We had fun creating this book. We enjoyed testing the recipes with our families and each other. And now, we hope you take pleasure in the moments you create as you entertain your family and guests with the themes and menus of **Tuxedos to Tailgates.**

PROFESSIONAL CREDITS

DESIGN AND ART
DIRECTION

Pamela Glick Creative
Pamela Glick

PHOTOGRAPHY

Phillip Esparza Photography
Phillip Esparza

FOOD STYLIST

Brooke Leonard

Spring

ॐ

OUR LIVES ARE NOT IN THE LAP OF THE GODS,
BUT IN THE LAP OF OUR COOKS.

—Lin Yutang in *The Importance of Living*

In the spring, everything is fresh and new. As the earth is rejuvenated, so are our thoughts and minds. We enjoy the beauty of our gardens as the trees start to bud. We watch as the first wildflowers of the year begin to bloom. As the weather warms and the sun begins to shine a bit brighter, we enjoy the laughter of friends who join us in celebrating spring.

The menus on the following pages honor the freshness of spring. Share a cozy moment with friends and loved ones at the Mom's Tea. Predict which celebrities will win at the Oscar Party. Join the excitement of a Bridesmaids' Luncheon. Simply take pleasure in good friends and good food at the Spring Buffet. Enjoy!

SPRING BUFFET

Celebrate spring with friends and family with this fresh and delectable menu.

Artichoke Brie Spread

SERVES 10 TO 12

2 (6-ounce) jars marinated artichoke
   hearts, drained
8 ounces cream cheese, softened
1 cup mayonnaise
3 tablespoons chopped green onions, or to
   taste
1/2 teaspoon oregano

1/2 teaspoon salt
3/4 teaspoon pepper
2 (4-ounce) packages Brie cheese,
   cut into small pieces

Garnish:
chopped fresh parsley

DIRECTIONS:

Preheat the oven to 375 degrees.

   Reserve 1 artichoke heart. Chop the remaining artichoke hearts coarsely in a large bowl. Add the cream cheese, mayonnaise, green onions, oregano, salt and pepper and mix well. Stir in the Brie cheese. Spoon into a greased 9-inch pie plate or baking dish.

   Bake for 15 to 20 minutes or until bubbly.

   To garnish, cut the reserved artichoke heart into halves. Arrange on top of the spread and sprinkle with parsley.

   Serve hot with crackers or bread.

Very Quick Dill Rolls

SERVES 8

1/4 cup (1/2 stick) butter, melted
1 tablespoon finely chopped onion

1 teaspoon dill weed
1 (10-count) can buttermilk biscuits

DIRECTIONS:

Preheat the oven to 450 degrees.

   Mix the butter, onion and dill weed in a bowl.

   Cut the biscuits into quarters or halves, depending on the size of the roll desired. Shape into balls. Dredge in the butter mixture. Arrange in a shallow baking pan.

   Bake for 8 minutes.

Spinach, Strawberry and Gorgonzola Salad

SERVES 6

1/2 small red onion, thinly sliced
4 cups water
24 walnut or pecan halves
2 tablespoons confectioners' sugar
2/3 cup vegetable oil
6 tablespoons walnut oil
2 small shallots or chives, minced

2 tablespoons raspberry, red wine or
  sherry vinegar
salt and freshly ground white pepper
  to taste
12 ounces fresh spinach, trimmed
1 pint strawberries, sliced
6 ounces gorgonzola cheese, crumbled

DIRECTIONS:

Place the onion in a small glass or stainless steel bowl. Add enough cold water to cover. Chill, covered with plastic wrap, for 30 minutes or longer.

Bring 4 cups water to a boil in a small saucepan. Plunge the walnuts into the boiling water. Boil for 30 seconds. Remove with a slotted spoon to a small bowl. Add the confectioners' sugar and toss until the walnuts are well glazed.

Heat the vegetable oil in a small skillet over medium-high heat. Drop the walnuts carefully into the hot vegetable oil, keeping the walnuts separated. Sauté for 1 to 2 minutes or until dark golden brown. Remove to a wire rack lined with parchment paper to cool.

Heat the walnut oil in a small saucepan over medium heat. Add the shallots. Sauté for 2 minutes or until translucent. Remove from the heat. Add the vinegar, salt and white pepper. (Do not overseason with salt as the cheese is salty also.) Whisk until lightly emulsified.

Tear the spinach into bite-size pieces into a large bowl. Drain the onion. Add the onion, strawberries and cheese and toss to mix well. Drizzle the dressing over the top and toss until lightly coated. Divide among salad plates and top with the candied walnuts.

Note: For an elegant entrée salad, add chicken. To prepare the chicken, arrange 2 boneless skinless chicken breasts in a shallow baking pan. Cover with 2 cups chicken broth. Bake, covered with foil, in a preheated 350-degree oven for 30 to 40 minutes or until cooked through. Remove from the oven and cool in the liquid. (The chicken can be baked up to 2 days ahead and chilled in the liquid. Return to room temperature before serving.) Cut into bite-size pieces or shred before serving.

The walnuts may be candied up to a week in advance and stored in an airtight container or in the freezer.

PHOTOGRAPH ON PAGE 19

Asparagus with Roasted Yellow Bell Pepper Sauce

To test baking powder for freshness, mix 2 tablespoons of the baking powder in 1 cup of water. If there is an immediate foaming and fizzing reaction, the baking powder is fresh. If the reaction is weak or delayed, throw it out and buy a new can.

SERVES 8

2 large yellow bell peppers
1/4 cup olive oil
1 tablespoon fresh lemon juice

salt and pepper to taste
2 pounds asparagus, trimmed
1 tablespoon olive oil

DIRECTIONS:

Char the bell peppers over a gas flame or broiler until blackened on all sides. Wrap in a paper bag and let stand for 10 minutes. Peel, seed and chop the bell peppers.

Purée the bell peppers and 1/4 cup olive oil in a blender. Add the lemon juice and blend until smooth. Season with salt and pepper.

Cook the asparagus in boiling water to cover in a large saucepan for 4 minutes or until tender-crisp; drain. Plunge immediately into a bowl of ice water to stop the cooking process. Cool and drain.

(The sauce and asparagus can be prepared up to 6 hours ahead. Cover and let stand at room temperature.)

Toss the asparagus with 1 tablespoon olive oil in a bowl. Season with salt and pepper. Arrange on a serving platter. Spoon some of the sauce over the top. Serve with the remaining sauce.

PHOTOGRAPH ON PAGE 31

Carrot Soufflé

SERVES 8

1 pound carrots, sliced
salt to taste
1/2 cup (1 stick) margarine, melted
1 teaspoon vanilla extract

3 eggs
1 cup sugar
3 tablespoons flour
1 teaspoon baking powder

DIRECTIONS:

Preheat the oven to 350 degrees.

Cook the carrots in boiling salted water to cover in a saucepan until tender; drain.

Process the carrots and margarine in a food processor until smooth. Add the vanilla, eggs, sugar, flour and baking powder and blend well. Spoon into a greased 1- or 2-quart baking dish.

Bake for 45 minutes or until firm.

Grilled Leg of Lamb

1 (6-pound) leg of lamb, boned and
    butterflied
1 cup olive oil
3/4 cup fresh lemon juice
1/4 cup chopped fresh parsley
2 teaspoons salt
1 1/2 teaspoons sage
1 1/2 teaspoons rosemary

1 1/2 teaspoons thyme
1/2 teaspoon freshly ground pepper
4 garlic cloves, crushed
2 bay leaves
Burgundy Sauce (below)

Garnish:
sprigs of fresh parsley

DIRECTIONS:

Arrange the lamb in a nonmetallic dish. Mix the olive oil, lemon juice, parsley, salt, sage, rosemary, thyme, pepper, garlic and bay leaves in a bowl. Pour over the lamb, turning to coat.

Marinate, covered, in the refrigerator for 24 hours, turning occasionally. Drain, reserving the marinade.

Place the lamb on a grill rack. Sear the lamb on both sides over hot coals. Reduce the heat to medium. Grill for 45 minutes, turning and basting with the reserved marinade frequently.

Remove the lamb to a heated serving platter and cover with foil. Let stand for 10 to 15 minutes. Cut into slices.

Arrange the slices on a serving platter. Drizzle with Burgundy Sauce. Garnish with parsley.

Burgundy Sauce

1/2 cup beef broth
1/3 cup red burgundy
2 tablespoons chopped shallots
1 1/2 teaspoons sage, finely chopped

1 1/2 teaspoons rosemary, finely chopped
1 1/2 teaspoons thyme, finely chopped
3 tablespoons butter, softened
3 tablespoons chopped fresh parsley

DIRECTIONS:

Bring the broth, burgundy, shallots and herbs to a boil in a saucepan. Boil until reduced by 1/2, stirring constantly. Remove from the heat.

Stir in the butter and parsley.

Chocolate Praline Layer Cake

For a beautiful garnish, decorate
your dishes with edible flowers.

SERVES 12

1/2 cup (1 stick) butter
1/4 cup whipping cream
1 cup packed brown sugar
1 cup coarsely chopped pecans
1 (2-layer) package devil's food
    cake mix
1 1/4 cups water
1/3 cup vegetable oil

3 eggs
1 3/4 cups whipping cream
1/4 cup confectioners' sugar
1/4 teaspoon vanilla extract

Garnishes:
pecan halves
chocolate curls

DIRECTIONS:

Preheat the oven to 325 degrees.

Combine the butter, 1/4 cup whipping cream and brown sugar in a small heavy saucepan. Cook over low heat until the butter is melted, stirring occasionally. Pour into two 8- or 9-inch cake pans. Sprinkle evenly with the chopped pecans.

Combine the cake mix, water, oil and eggs in a large mixing bowl and blend at low speed until moistened. Beat at high speed for 2 minutes. Spoon carefully into the prepared pans.

Bake for 35 to 45 minutes or until the cake springs back when lightly touched in the center. Cool in the pans for 5 minutes. Remove from the pans to wire racks to cool completely.

Beat 1 3/4 cups whipping cream in a mixing bowl until soft peaks form. Add the confectioners' sugar and vanilla and beat until stiff peaks form.

To assemble, arrange 1 cake layer praline side up on a serving plate. Spread with 1/2 of the topping. Top with the remaining layer praline side up. Spread with the remaining topping. Garnish with pecan halves and chocolate curls. Store in the refrigerator.

Orange Cake

1 (2-layer) package yellow cake mix
1 (3-ounce) package orange gelatin
1 teaspoon orange extract
1 cup confectioners' sugar

2 to 3 tablespoons orange juice
1/2 teaspoon orange zest (optional)
1/4 teaspoon vanilla extract (optional)

DIRECTIONS:

Prepare the cake mix using the package directions, adding the gelatin and orange extract. Bake using the package directions. Cool completely.

Combine the confectioners' sugar, orange juice, orange zest and vanilla in a bowl and beat until smooth. Brush or drizzle over the cooled cake.

Note: Prepare 1 to 2 days ahead of time to enhance the flavor. Double the recipe for the glaze if the cake is baked in a large bundt pan.

Spring Spritzer

1 (1.5-liter) bottle white wine, chilled
1 (1-liter) bottle sparkling water, chilled

1 lemon, thinly sliced

DIRECTIONS:

Fill each glass almost half full of wine. Add enough sparkling water to fill the glass. Add a twist of lemon.

Note: You may use one 49-ounce bottle of cranberry juice cocktail instead of the wine.

OSCAR PARTY

The night of the Academy Awards is the biggest night in Hollywood. Why not treat your friends to a glamorous evening—but in front of the TV? This menu is comprised of easy-to-eat fare and finger foods that will allow your guests to enjoy appetizing treats while watching the evening unfold.

Mock Champagne

MAKES 16 (½-CUP) SERVINGS

1 (6-ounce) can frozen lemonade
  concentrate, thawed
3/4 cup pineapple juice
1 (6-ounce) can frozen white grape juice,
  thawed

2 cups cold water
1 3/4 cups ginger ale, chilled
1 3/4 cups sparkling water, chilled

DIRECTIONS:

Combine the lemonade concentrate, pineapple juice, grape juice and water in a 2-quart pitcher and mix well. Chill, covered, until ready to serve. Stir in the ginger ale and sparkling water just before serving.

Hot Crab Dip

MAKES 3⅔ CUPS

3/4 cup sour cream
2 tablespoons fresh lemon juice
1 tablespoon grated onion
1 teaspoon Worcestershire sauce
3/4 teaspoon dry mustard
1/4 teaspoon garlic powder

8 ounces cream cheese, softened
1/2 cup (2 ounces) shredded sharp
  Cheddar cheese
1 pound lump crab meat, drained and
  shells removed
paprika to taste

DIRECTIONS:

Preheat the oven to 325 degrees.

Whisk the sour cream, lemon juice, onion, Worcestershire sauce, dry mustard, garlic powder and cream cheese in a bowl until smooth. Stir in the Cheddar cheese and crab meat. Spoon into a 1 1/2-quart baking dish sprayed with nonstick cooking spray. Sprinkle with paprika.

Bake for 30 minutes or until heated through.

Serve warm with crackers or breadsticks.

Note: You may use fat-free sour cream and light cream cheese.

Cheesy Crescent Puffs

MAKES 2 DOZEN

1 (8-count) can crescent rolls
8 ounces Pepper Jack cheese or
    mozzarella cheese

1/4 cup Italian salad dressing
2 1/2 ounces sesame seeds
1 cup grated Parmesan cheese

DIRECTIONS:

Preheat the oven to 375 degrees.

Unroll the crescent roll dough and separate into triangles. Cut each triangle into thirds. Cut the Pepper Jack cheese into 24 cubes.

Wrap each cube in the dough, sealing to enclose. Dip in the salad dressing. Roll in the sesame seeds and Parmesan cheese. Place in greased muffin cups.

Bake for 15 to 18 minutes or until golden brown.

Use a bit of fresh lemon juice to remove the smell of onion from your hands.

Caramel Popcorn

SERVES 12

6 quarts popped unseasoned popcorn
1 cup (2 sticks) butter
2 cups packed brown sugar

1/2 cup light corn syrup
1/2 teaspoon baking soda
1 teaspoon vanilla extract

DIRECTIONS:

Preheat the oven to 250 degrees.

Layer the popcorn in two 9×13-inch baking pans.

Bring the butter, brown sugar and corn syrup to a boil in a saucepan over high heat. Boil for 5 minutes. Remove from the heat. Stir in the baking soda and vanilla. Pour over the popcorn.

Bake for 1 hour, stirring every 15 minutes. Invert the popcorn onto waxed paper to cool.

Store in an airtight container.

Onion Rye Appetizers

MAKES 20 TO 24 APPETIZERS

1 (2-ounce) can French-fried onions, crushed
1 (2-ounce) jar crumbled bacon, or 3/4 cup cooked bacon bits
1/2 cup mayonnaise
3 cups (12 ounces) shredded Swiss cheese
1 (14-ounce) jar pizza sauce
1 (16-ounce) loaf snack rye bread

DIRECTIONS:

Preheat the oven to 350 degrees.

Combine the onions, bacon, mayonnaise and cheese in a small bowl and stir to mix well.

Spread about 1 teaspoon pizza sauce on each slice of bread. Top each with 1 tablespoon of the cheese mixture. Arrange in a single layer on an ungreased baking sheet.

Bake for 12 to 14 minutes or until the cheese is melted.

Note: To prepare ahead, freeze the unbaked appetizers on the baking sheet. Place in a plastic freezer bag and seal the bag. Store in the freezer for up to 2 months. To serve, arrange on a baking sheet. Bake in a preheated 350-degree oven for 14 to 16 minutes or until the cheese melts.

For an interesting centerpiece, place several glass candlesticks of varying heights on the table and decorate with seasonal touches—flowers in the spring, fresh herbs in the summer, autumn leaves in the fall, and holiday greenery in the winter.

Walnut and Avocado Salad

SERVES 8

1/3 cup white wine vinegar
1/2 teaspoon lemon juice
2/3 cup vegetable oil
1 garlic clove, minced
1 teaspoon salt
1/4 teaspoon pepper
1/2 head iceberg lettuce, torn
1/2 head romaine, torn
1 avocado, chopped
1/2 cup walnuts, toasted

DIRECTIONS:

Combine the vinegar, lemon juice, oil, garlic, salt and pepper in a cruet and shake to mix well. Chill for 2 to 24 hours.

Combine the iceberg lettuce, romaine, avocado and walnuts in a salad bowl and toss to mix well. Drizzle with the desired amount of salad dressing just before serving and toss to coat.

Home-Style Potatoes

5 cups cooked diced unpeeled
  new potatoes
1¹/2 tablespoons olive oil
1¹/2 tablespoons water
³/4 teaspoon paprika

¹/2 teaspoon garlic powder
¹/2 teaspoon black pepper
dash of cayenne pepper
pinch of salt
grated Parmesan cheese

DIRECTIONS:

Preheat the oven to 425 degrees.

Mix the potatoes, olive oil, water, paprika, garlic powder, black pepper, cayenne pepper and salt in a bowl with your hands. Spread on a baking sheet sprayed with nonstick cooking spray.

Bake for 30 minutes or until crispy. Sprinkle lightly with cheese.

Italian Beef Sandwiches

SERVES 10 TO 12

1 (5- to 6-pound) rolled cross rib
  beef roast
3 onions, chopped
1 tablespoon salt
1 teaspoon garlic salt

1 teaspoon oregano
1¹/2 teaspoons basil
1 tablespoon Italian seasoning
2 tablespoons MSG
1 (16-ounce) jar banana peppers

DIRECTIONS:

Preheat the oven to 325 degrees.

Arrange the beef on a rack in a roasting pan. Sprinkle with the onions.

Roast for 2¹/2 hours or until tender. Remove the beef from the oven to cool. Drain the beef, reserving the drippings. Cut the beef into thin slices and layer in a baking dish.

Combine the reserved drippings, salt, garlic salt, oregano, basil, Italian seasoning and MSG in a saucepan. Bring to a boil. Pour over the sliced beef. Add the banana peppers. Chill, covered, for 24 hours.

To serve, preheat the oven to 350 degrees. Bake for 35 minutes. Serve with Italian hard rolls.

Note: Add one 10-ounce can French onion soup if needed to supplement the beef drippings.

Bailey's Irish Cream Brownie Pie

1 (1-crust) pie pastry
1/2 cup (1 stick) butter
1/2 cup baking cocoa, or 1 ounce
　　unsweetened chocolate, melted
2 eggs
1 cup sugar

2 tablespoons Bailey's Irish cream
1 teaspoon vanilla extract
1/3 cup flour
1/4 teaspoon salt
1 cup chopped walnuts or pecans

DIRECTIONS:

Preheat the oven to 350 degrees.

Line a 9-inch pie plate with the pastry, forming a high edge. Trim and flute the edge. Chill while preparing the filling.

Melt the butter with the baking cocoa in a small heavy saucepan over medium-low heat. Remove from the heat and cool slightly.

Beat the eggs in a small mixing bowl at high speed until foamy. Beat in the sugar gradually in a fine stream until the eggs are thick and pale yellow. Reduce the speed to low. Beat in the chocolate mixture, liqueur and vanilla. Fold in a mixture of the flour and salt.

Sprinkle the walnuts over the pie pastry. Pour the filling over the walnuts.

Bake for 30 minutes or until the crust is golden brown and the filling is set. Remove to a wire rack to cool.

Serve with ice cream or whipped cream flavored with additional Bailey's Irish cream.

PHOTOGRAPH RIGHT:
SPINACH, STRAWBERRY AND GORGONZOLA SALAD

TAX DAY SUPPER

For most Americans, April 15 represents one of two opposites: an inflow or an outflow of cash. Both are great reasons to gather with friends, either to celebrate or to mourn your losses. To commemorate this yearly event, we bring you our Rich Man/Poor Man menus. Either way, you will enjoy a delicious dinner.

RICH MAN

Mixed Field Greens with Goat Cheese and Raspberry Vinaigrette

SERVES 4

2 slices white bread
4 ounces goat cheese
1/4 cup sliced almonds
1/4 cup pecan pieces

2 cups chopped Granny Smith apples
8 ounces mixed field greens
1 cup Raspberry Vinaigrette (page 21)
1 tablespoon butter

DIRECTIONS:

Tear the bread into small pieces and place in a food processor. Pulse to form coarse bread crumbs. Spread evenly on a plate. Divide the cheese into 4 equal portions. Shape each portion into a ball. Roll in the bread crumbs to coat and flatten into small patties. Chill, covered, in the refrigerator.

Preheat the oven to 300 degrees.

Sprinkle the almonds and pecans in a small baking pan.

Bake for 10 minutes.

Combine the apples, mixed greens and Raspberry Vinaigrette in a large salad bowl and toss to coat. Divide the salad among 4 serving plates.

Melt the butter in a nonstick skillet over medium heat. Add the cheese patties. Cook for 1 minute on each side. Arrange 1 patty on each salad. Sprinkle with the toasted almonds and pecans.

Raspberry Vinaigrette

⟡

Makes 2 cups

1/4 cup raspberry preserves	1/2 teaspoon fresh tarragon, minced
2 tablespoons chopped purple onion	1/4 cup fresh lemon juice
1/2 teaspoon minced garlic	pinch of salt
1/2 cup white wine vinegar	pinch of pepper
1/2 teaspoon fresh oregano, minced	1 cup olive oil

DIRECTIONS:

Process the preserves, onion, garlic, vinegar, oregano, tarragon, lemon juice, salt, pepper and 1/2 of the olive oil in a blender until smooth. Pour into a medium bowl.

Add the remaining olive oil in a fine stream, whisking constantly.

Fire-Roasted Beef Tenderloin

⟡

Serves 4

1/2 cup peanut oil	1 tablespoon honey
1 tablespoon black peppercorns	1/2 cup madeira
1 tablespoon ground star anise	3/4 cup beef stock
1 teaspoon coriander seeds	1 pound beef tenderloin
1/4 teaspoon Szechuan peppercorns	1 1/2 teaspoons Chinese powdered mustard
1/2 teaspoon red curry paste	1 tablespoon rice wine vinegar
1 tablespoon tamarind paste	2 tablespoons butter

DIRECTIONS:

Preheat the grill. Preheat the oven to 400 degrees.

Heat the peanut oil, black peppercorns, ground star anise, coriander seeds and Szechuan peppercorns in a saucepan for 1 minute or until aromatic. Stir in the red curry paste, tamarind paste and honey. Add the wine, stirring to deglaze the saucepan. Cook until the mixture is reduced to a syrupy consistency. Add the beef stock. Continue to cook until the mixture is reduced by 1/2. Purée in a blender. Strain the mixture, discarding the solids.

Place the beef on a grill rack. Grill until grill marks appear on all sides. Arrange in a baking pan. Add 1/2 of the strained sauce. Roast in the oven for 4 to 5 minutes or to the desired degree of doneness.

Pour the remaining sauce into a saucepan. Cook over medium heat until thickened, stirring frequently.

Dissolve the Chinese powdered mustard in the vinegar in a small bowl. Whisk into the sauce. Add the butter and whisk until melted.

To serve, cut the beef into thin slices and arrange on a platter. Serve with the mustard sauce.

For an easy centerpiece, fill three clear, tall glass vases with different levels of glass marbles. Fill the vases with water until almost full. You can use clear or colored marbles—the clear will be a bit more formal while the colored ones add a festive touch.

Wasabi Mashed Potatoes

SERVES 4

1 pound baking potatoes, such as russet
   potatoes
salt to taste
1/4 cup (1/2 stick) butter, cut into pieces
1/4 cup heavy cream, heated

1 tablespoon roasted garlic purée
8 ounces spinach, trimmed
1 1/2 teaspoons wasabi powder
pepper to taste

DIRECTIONS:

Peel the potatoes and cut into large pieces of equal size. Place in a saucepan with enough salted water to cover. Bring to a boil. Cook the potatoes until tender; drain. Force through a food mill. Whip in the butter, hot cream and garlic purée.

Blanch the spinach in enough boiling salted water to cover in a saucepan for 10 seconds. Plunge immediately into ice water in a bowl to stop the cooking process; drain thoroughly.

Process the spinach and wasabi powder in a blender until puréed. Stir into the mashed potatoes. Season with salt and pepper.

Almond Joy Cake

SERVES 30

1 (2-layer) package chocolate cake mix
1 cup evaporated milk
1 cup sugar
24 large marshmallows
1 (14-ounce) can shredded coconut

1/2 cup evaporated milk
1 1/2 cups sugar
1/2 cup (1 stick) margarine
2 cups (12 ounces) chocolate chips
1 cup slivered almonds

DIRECTIONS:

Preheat the oven to 350 degrees.

Prepare the cake mix using the package directions. Pour into 2 greased and floured 9×13-inch cake pans. Bake for 15 to 20 minutes or until the layers test done. Remove from the oven to cool.

Bring 1 cup evaporated milk and 1 cup sugar to a boil in a saucepan. Boil for 2 to 3 minutes, stirring constantly. Stir in the marshmallows until melted. Remove from the heat. Add the coconut and mix well. Let stand until cool.

Bring 1/2 cup evaporated milk, 1 1/2 cups sugar and the margarine to a boil in a saucepan. Remove from the heat. Add the chocolate chips and stir until smooth. Stir in the almonds. Let stand until cool.

Spread the coconut mixture over the cake layers. Spread chocolate icing evenly over the coconut mixture. Chill, covered, until ready to serve.

POOR MAN

For casual place cards, write your guests' names with a silver paint pen on large flat river rocks.

Corn and Black Bean Salsa

MAKES 5 CUPS

1 (16-ounce) can whole kernel sweet
   corn, drained
1 (16-ounce) can black beans, rinsed
   and drained
1/2 cup chopped fresh cilantro
1/4 cup chopped red onion
1/4 cup chopped green onions

1/3 cup fresh lime juice
3 tablespoons vegetable oil
1 tablespoon cumin
salt and pepper to taste
1/2 cup chopped seeded tomatoes
1 avocado, chopped

DIRECTIONS:

Combine the corn, black beans, cilantro, red onion, green onions, lime juice, oil and cumin in a large bowl and mix well. Season with salt and pepper.

Chill, covered, for at least 1 hour or up to 12 hours. Add the tomatoes and avocado just before serving. Serve with corn chips or pita toasts.

Pita Toasts

SERVES 6 TO 8

1/2 cup (1 stick) butter, softened
2 teaspoons lemon pepper

2 teaspoons cumin
6 pita bread pockets

DIRECTIONS:

Preheat the oven to 350 degrees.

Combine the butter, lemon pepper and cumin in a bowl and mix well.

Separate the pita pockets into halves. Cut each half into triangles. Spread with the butter mixture. Arrange on a baking sheet.

Bake for 8 to 12 minutes or until crisp.

Taxpayers' Chicken Chili

6 large chicken breasts
3 tablespoons vegetable oil
3 onions, coarsely chopped
6 garlic cloves, minced
1 jalapeño chile, minced
1/4 cup chili powder
3 tablespoons cumin
1 tablespoon oregano

2 teaspoons coriander
1 (28-ounce) can crushed tomatoes in
    purée
2 (12-ounce) bottles beer
2 1/2 cups canned reduced-sodium chicken
    broth
2 (15-ounce) cans kidney beans, rinsed
    and drained

DIRECTIONS:

Arrange the chicken in a single layer in a large skillet. Add enough water to cover. Bring to a boil and reduce the heat. Simmer, covered, for 12 minutes or until the chicken is cooked through. Drain the chicken and cool slightly. Shred the chicken coarsely, discarding the skin and bones. (You may prepare 1 day ahead and chill, covered, in the refrigerator.)

Heat the oil in a large heavy stockpot over medium-high heat. Add the onions. Sauté for 10 minutes or until tender. Add the garlic and jalapeño chile. Sauté for 1 minute. Stir in the chili powder, cumin, oregano and coriander. Add the tomatoes, beer and broth.

Bring to a simmer over medium-low heat. Simmer for 1 hour to blend the flavors, stirring occasionally.

Add the kidney beans. Simmer, uncovered, for 30 minutes or until the chili thickens, stirring occasionally. Add the chicken. Simmer until heated through.

Ladle into serving bowls. Serve with salsa, chips, green onions, sour cream and shredded Cheddar cheese.

Lime Ice Cream

SERVES 4

2 cups heavy cream
1 cup sugar

2 teaspoons grated lime zest
1/3 cup fresh lime juice

When entertaining a large number of guests, invite a friend over an hour early to help you with last minute preparations.

DIRECTIONS:

Combine the cream and sugar in a large bowl and mix until the sugar is dissolved. Stir in the lime zest and lime juice. (The mixture will begin to thicken slightly.)

Pour into a freezer-safe metal or plastic container and cover with foil. Freeze for 4 hours or until firm.

Scoop or spoon into individual serving bowls. Serve with sliced fruit, such as mango, blueberries, kiwifruit or strawberries.

Brown Sugar Cookies

MAKES ABOUT 6 DOZEN

1/2 cup plus 2 tablespoons flour
1/4 teaspoon cinnamon
pinch of salt
pinch of nutmeg

1/4 cup (1/2 stick) unsalted butter, softened
1/4 cup packed dark brown sugar
1/4 cup packed light brown sugar
2 egg whites, beaten until frothy

DIRECTIONS:

Preheat the oven to 400 degrees.

Sift the flour, cinnamon, salt and nutmeg together. Cream the butter and brown sugar in a mixing bowl until light and fluffy. Add the egg whites and beat until blended. Add the flour mixture. Beat at low speed until blended.

Spoon the batter into a pastry bag fitted with a 1/4-inch plain or star tip. Pipe 2-inch lengths 2 1/2 inches apart onto a buttered cookie sheet.

Bake for 5 minutes or until the edges are light brown. Cool for 2 minutes on the cookie sheet. Remove to a wire rack to cool completely.

Note: Great served with ice cream.

MOM'S TEA

Show all the mothers you know how much you appreciate them with this scrumptious "ladies'" menu. You will find the best of High Tea—delicate finger sandwiches, fresh scones, and more.

Tea Punch

MAKES 4½ QUARTS

1 (12-ounce) can frozen orange juice concentrate, thawed
1 (12-ounce) can frozen lemonade concentrate, thawed
3 cups apple cider or cranapple juice
6 cups water
3 tablespoons instant tea granules

1/2 cup sugar
juice of 1 lemon
1 quart ginger ale, chilled

Garnishes:
sprigs of fresh mint
fresh fruit

DIRECTIONS:

Combine the orange juice concentrate, lemonade concentrate, apple cider, water, tea granules, sugar and lemon juice in a large pitcher and mix well.

Chill, covered, until ready to serve.

To serve, stir in the ginger ale. Garnish with mint and fresh fruit.

Scotch Shortbread

MAKES 6 TO 8 DOZEN

2 cups (4 sticks) butter, softened
1/2 cup packed brown sugar
1/2 cup confectioners' sugar

51/2 cups flour
1/2 teaspoon vanilla extract

DIRECTIONS:

Preheat the oven to 275 degrees.

Cream the butter in a mixing bowl. Add the brown sugar and confectioners' sugar and beat until light and fluffy. Add the flour and vanilla and blend well.

Roll the dough on a pastry cloth or board 1/4 inch thick. Cut into 2-inch squares or 2- to 3-inch circles. Arrange on ungreased cookie sheets.

Bake for 1 hour.

Gorgonzola and Pear Tea Sandwiches

2 tablespoons cream cheese, softened
1/2 cup Gorgonzola cheese, crumbled
2 tablespoons heavy cream

8 thin slices raisin pumpernickel bread
2 pears, peeled and thinly sliced

DIRECTIONS:

Combine the cream cheese, Gorgonzola cheese and cream in a bowl and mix to blend well.

Spread the cheese mixture on 1/2 of the bread slices. Top with the pear slices, remaining cheese mixture and remaining bread slices.

Tomato and Sour Cream Tea Sandwiches

2 ounces cream cheese, softened
1/4 cup sour cream
1 tablespoon oregano, chopped

salt and pepper to taste
8 thin slices firm white bread
2 tomatoes, cut into thin slices

DIRECTIONS:

Combine the cream cheese, sour cream and oregano in a small bowl and mix well. Season with salt and pepper.

Trim the crusts from the bread slices. Spread the cream cheese mixture on the bread slices. Arrange the tomatoes on 1/2 of the bread slices. Top with the remaining bread slices.

Cut each sandwich into 3 equal strips.

Smoked Salmon Tea Sandwiches

When serving on a silver tray, line the tray with leafy green lettuce. Not only will it serve as a garnish, but it will protect the tray from acidic juices.

MAKES 2 DOZEN

1/2 cup (1 stick) unsalted butter, softened
2 ounces cream cheese, softened
1 tablespoon grated fresh gingerroot
1 tablespoon fresh lime juice

3 tablespoons chopped fresh cilantro
1 teaspoon kosher salt
24 slices thin white bread
8 ounces thinly sliced smoked salmon

DIRECTIONS:

Process the butter, cream cheese, gingerroot, lime juice, cilantro and kosher salt in a food processor for 30 seconds or until combined. Shape into a 10-inch log 1 1/2 inches wide on a sheet of parchment paper or waxed paper and roll up in the paper, sealing the ends. Chill until ready to serve.

Spread the bread slices generously with the ginger butter. Arrange the smoked salmon in an even layer on 1/2 of the bread slices. Top with the remaining bread slices.

Cut each sandwich with a 2-inch flower-shaped cookie cutter. Remove the top slice of bread from each flower. Cut a circle from the center of each with a 3/4- to 7/8-inch round biscuit cutter, discarding the circle. Replace the bread slice, buttered side down, on the flower.

Lemon Cream Cheese Scones

2¼ cups flour
¼ cup sugar
1 tablespoon grated lemon zest
2 teaspoons baking powder
¼ teaspoon salt
⅓ cup butter or margarine

3 ounces cream cheese, softened
1 egg
⅓ cup milk
lemon juice for brushing
sugar to taste

DIRECTIONS:

Preheat the oven to 400 degrees.

Mix the flour, ¼ cup sugar, lemon zest, baking powder and salt in a large bowl. Cut in the butter with a pastry blender until crumbly.

Mix the cream cheese and egg in a small bowl until smooth. Add the milk gradually, stirring constantly. Stir into the flour mixture until the mixture forms a ball and leaves the side of the bowl.

Drop by spoonfuls about 2 inches apart onto an ungreased baking sheet. Brush with lemon juice and sprinkle with sugar.

Bake for 16 to 18 minutes or until golden brown. Remove immediately from the baking sheet and serve warm.

Orange Brandy Butter

SERVES 20

1¼ cups (2½ sticks) unsalted butter, softened
2½ cups confectioners' sugar, sifted
¼ cup ground almonds

Finely grated zest of 1 orange
1 tablespoon strained orange juice
1 to 2 tablespoons brandy (optional)

DIRECTIONS:

Beat the butter and confectioners' sugar in a mixing bowl until creamy. Add the almonds and beat well. Stir in the orange zest and orange juice. Stir in the brandy. Pack into small butter dishes or a crock. Chill or freeze until ready to serve.

Dried Blueberry Almond Scones

To save time on the day of your event, cut and measure all of your ingredients. Dry ingredients can be mixed ahead of time, placed in a sealable plastic bag, and labeled so that all you need to do before the party is dump the ingredients and mix.

SERVES 10

2 cups flour	1/2 cup milk
1/4 cup sugar	1 egg, lightly beaten
1 tablespoon baking powder	1 teaspoon almond extract
1/4 cup (1/2 stick) unsalted butter, chilled and cut into pieces	3/4 cup dried blueberries
	1/4 cup sliced almonds

DIRECTIONS:

Preheat the oven to 350 degrees.

Whisk the flour, sugar and baking powder in a bowl. Cut in the butter using a pastry blender until the mixture resembles coarse crumbs. Add 2/3 of the milk, egg and almond extract and stir until smooth. Stir in the blueberries and almonds.

Roll or pat the dough into a disk of medium thickness on a lightly floured surface. Cut into 10 equal wedges. Arrange on lightly greased baking sheets. Brush the tops with the remaining milk.

Bake for 20 minutes or until light brown. Serve warm.

Strawberry Flowers

MAKES 32

32 medium strawberries	1/4 teaspoon almond extract
11 ounces cream cheese, softened	2 tablespoons grated semisweet chocolate
3 tablespoons confectioners' sugar	

DIRECTIONS:

Cut a thin slice from the stem end of each strawberry, allowing the berries to stand upright. Place cut side down on a serving platter. Cut each into 4 wedges to but not through the bottom. Fan the wedges slightly.

Beat the cream cheese, confectioners' sugar and almond extract in a mixing bowl at medium speed until light and fluffy. Fold in the chocolate. Spoon into a pastry bag fitted with a large star tip.

Pipe the cream cheese mixture into the center of each berry. Chill until ready to serve.

PHOTOGRAPH RIGHT:
ASPARAGUS WITH ROASTED YELLOW BELL PEPPER SAUCE

Raspberry and White Chocolate Cheesecake

Slice cheesecake by using tautly held dental floss.

SERVES 12

2¼ cups coarsely broken chocolate wafer
  cookies
6 tablespoons unsalted butter, melted
1 (12-ounce) package frozen unsweetened
  raspberries, thawed
6 ounces white chocolate, finely chopped
32 ounces cream cheese, softened
1⅓ cups sugar

2 tablespoons flour
4 eggs
2 tablespoons whipping cream
2 teaspoons vanilla extract
½ teaspoon almond extract

Garnish:
white chocolate curls

DIRECTIONS:

Preheat the oven to 325 degrees.

Butter a 9-inch springform pan. Double wrap the outside of the pan with heavy-duty foil.

Process the cookies in a food processor to form coarse crumbs. Add the butter and process until evenly moistened. Press firmly onto the bottom and halfway up the side of the prepared pan.

Bake for 8 minutes. Cool on a wire rack.

Press the undrained raspberries through a fine strainer into a small bowl. Measure ½ cup of the purée and reserve the remaining purée for another use.

Melt the white chocolate in a double boiler over barely simmering water, stirring constantly.

Beat the cream cheese and sugar in a large mixing bowl until smooth and fluffy. Add the flour and beat well. Add the eggs 1 at a time, beating well after each addition. Beat in the whipping cream and vanilla.

Combine 2¼ cups of the batter and the melted white chocolate in a medium bowl and mix well.

Add the raspberry purée and almond extract to the remaining batter and mix well. Pour into the prepared pan. Place the springform pan in a large roasting pan. Pour enough hot water into the roasting pan to come 1 inch up the side of the springform pan.

Bake for 50 to 70 minutes or until the raspberry mixture is softly set in the center and beginning to puff at the edge. Remove the roasting pan from the oven. Cool for 5 minutes or until slightly firm.

Spoon the white chocolate batter into concentric circles onto the raspberry layer, beginning at the edge of the pan. Smooth the top.

Bake for 30 to 40 minutes or until the white chocolate layer is set in the center. Chill, uncovered, for 4 hours or longer. (You may prepare 2 days ahead of time and chill, covered, until ready to serve.)

To serve, loosen the cheesecake from the side of the pan with a small knife and release the side of the pan. Garnish with white chocolate curls.

GRADUATION GRILL

Honor your favorite graduate by throwing a casual outdoor party to commemorate his or her achievement. This menu is sure to appeal to graduates and guests of all ages. Enjoy!

Crispy Vegetable Chips

SERVES 4 TO 6

1/4 cup unbleached flour
1/2 teaspoon oregano
1/4 teaspoon garlic powder
1/8 teaspoon red pepper
2 egg whites

2 tablespoons water
2/3 cup cornflake crumbs
1/4 cup grated Parmesan cheese
3 cups sliced vegetables, such as zucchini, yellow squash or carrots

DIRECTIONS:

Preheat the oven to 350 degrees.

Combine the flour, oregano, garlic powder and red pepper in a sealable plastic bag and shake to mix well.

Whisk the egg whites and water in a pie plate.

Combine the cornflake crumbs and cheese in a sealable plastic bag and shake to mix well.

Add the vegetables to the flour mixture and shake until coated. Dip the vegetables in the egg white mixture. Add to the cornflake mixture and shake until coated. Arrange in a single layer on a baking sheet sprayed with nonstick cooking spray.

Bake for 10 minutes. Turn the slices. Bake for 8 minutes longer or until golden brown.

Serve with ranch salad dressing for dipping.

Menu

CRISPY VEGETABLE CHIPS

■

SUMMER TOMATO SALAD

■

ROASTED CORN

■

SESAME GRILLED ASPARAGUS

■

GREAT CHEESEBURGERS

■

GRILLED CHICKEN SANDWICHES WITH ROASTED RED PEPPERS AND ARUGULA

■

SINFUL BROWNIES

■

MUD PIE

Summer Tomato Salad

SERVES 6

1 pound tomatoes, chopped
1/3 cup chopped green or black Greek
    olives (kalamata)
1/4 cup chopped fresh parsley
1 tablespoon wine vinegar
1/4 cup olive oil

1/2 cup chopped purple or sweet onion
1 medium garlic clove, chopped
1/4 cup chopped fresh basil, or
    1 1/4 tablespoons dried basil
salt and pepper to taste
crumbled feta cheese (optional)

DIRECTIONS:

Combine the tomatoes, olives, parsley, vinegar, olive oil, onion, garlic, basil, salt and pepper in a bowl and toss to mix well.

Sprinkle with cheese.

Serve at room temperature.

Note: For variety, add 16 ounces spaghetti, cooked and drained, and toss to mix well. Serve with shredded Parmesan cheese or cubes of fresh mozzarella cheese.

Roasted Corn

SERVES 8

1/2 cup (1 stick) butter
2 tablespoons finely chopped fresh chives
    or green onion tops
2 tablespoons chopped fresh parsley

8 ears of corn
salt and pepper to taste
dash of paprika

DIRECTIONS:

Preheat the grill.

Melt the butter with the chives and parsley in a small saucepan.

Pull back the husks carefully from the corn and remove the silks. Brush the corn with the butter mixture. Sprinkle with salt, pepper and paprika. Recover the corn with the husks. Place on a grill rack.

Grill over hot coals until tender, turning frequently.

Note: You may also wrap in foil and bake in a preheated 400-degree oven for 30 minutes.

Sesame Grilled Asparagus

SERVES 4 TO 6

1 pound asparagus
2 tablespoons dark sesame oil
1 tablespoon soy sauce

1 garlic clove, minced
salt and pepper to taste
2 tablespoons sesame seeds

DIRECTIONS:

Preheat the grill.

Trim the woody portion from the asparagus spears. Skewer 4 or 5 spears together with a wooden pick or bamboo skewers that have been soaked in water to prevent burning.

Combine the sesame oil, soy sauce and garlic in a small bowl and mix well. Brush on both sides of the skewered asparagus. Season with salt and pepper. Arrange on a grill rack.

Grill for 2 to 4 minutes per side or until brown, sprinkling with sesame seeds while grilling.

Serve warm.

To easily peel garlic, smash the clove lightly with the blade of your knife. The skin will peel right off.

Great Cheeseburgers

SERVES 10

2 pounds ground chuck
1 pound ground sirloin
3 tablespoons steak sauce
6 egg yolks

1 1/2 teaspoons salt
3/4 teaspoon freshly ground pepper
12 ounces white Cheddar cheese,
   thinly sliced

DIRECTIONS:

Preheat the grill.

Mix the ground chuck, ground sirloin, steak sauce, egg yolks, salt and pepper with a fork in a large bowl; do not mash. Divide into 10 equal portions and shape into patties. Arrange on a grill rack.

Grill for 5 minutes. Turn the patties and top with the cheese. Grill for 3 to 5 minutes longer or until cooked through. Remove to a plate and cover with foil. Let stand for 5 minutes before serving.

Grilled Chicken Sandwiches with Roasted Red Peppers and Arugula

SERVES 4

3 tablespoons mayonnaise
3 tablespoons nonfat yogurt
4 teaspoons Dijon mustard
1/2 cup chopped arugula
4 boneless chicken breasts
1 teaspoon olive oil
1 tablespoon chopped fresh rosemary
1 teaspoon oregano

dash of salt
dash of pepper
4 (6-inch) baguettes
arugula leaves
1 red bell pepper, roasted, cut into thin
    slices
2 tablespoons shredded Parmesan cheese

DIRECTIONS:

Preheat the grill.

Blend the mayonnaise, yogurt, Dijon mustard and chopped arugula in a bowl.

Brush the chicken lightly with the olive oil. Sprinkle with the rosemary, oregano, salt and pepper. Arrange on a grill rack.

Grill for 4 to 5 minutes per side or until cooked through. Cut the chicken into thin slices.

Cut the baguettes into halves. Spread the cut sides with the mayonnaise mixture. Arrange the arugula leaves on the bottom halves. Arrange the chicken and bell peppers over the arugula leaves. Sprinkle with the cheese. Replace the top halves.

Note: You may prepare up to 4 hours in advance.

Sinful Brownies

MAKES 1⅓ DOZEN

4 ounces unsweetened chocolate
1/2 cup (1 stick) margarine
2 cups sugar
4 eggs, beaten
1 cup flour
1 teaspoon vanilla extract

2 cups (12 ounces) chocolate chips
1 cup miniature marshmallows
1/2 cup chopped nuts (optional)
1 tablespoon Kahlúa, or to taste
chocolate chips
miniature marshmallows

DIRECTIONS:

Preheat the oven to 325 degrees.

Melt the chocolate and margarine in a double boiler over hot water. Cool slightly.

Beat the sugar and eggs in a mixing bowl until light and fluffy. Blend in the chocolate mixture. Stir in the flour. Add the vanilla, 2 cups chocolate chips, 1 cup marshmallows, nuts and Kahlúa and mix well. Spread in a greased 9×9-inch baking pan. Sprinkle with additional chocolate chips and marshmallows.

Bake for 35 to 45 minutes or until the brownies pull away from the edge of the pan. Remove from the oven and cool in the pan.

Decorate your home with fresh flowers whenever you entertain. Even a single daisy from your garden on the powder room vanity adds a special touch.

Mud Pie

Store coffee in the freezer to preserve its fresh flavor.

SERVES 12

1½ cups crushed cinnamon snaps
1 tablespoon margarine, melted
1 quart coffee frozen yogurt

6 ounces Bittersweet Fudge Sauce (below)
¼ cup slivered almonds, toasted

DIRECTIONS:

Mix the cookie crumbs and margarine in a bowl until moistened. Press into a 9-inch pie plate. Spoon the frozen yogurt into the prepared pie plate.

Freeze until firm. Top with the Bittersweet Fudge Sauce. Sprinkle with the almonds.

Bittersweet Fudge Sauce

MAKES 1½ CUPS

⅓ cup baking cocoa
⅓ cup packed brown sugar
1 tablespoon instant coffee granules

1 teaspoon cornstarch
⅔ cup evaporated skim milk
⅓ cup water

DIRECTIONS:

Combine the baking cocoa, brown sugar, coffee granules and cornstarch in a small saucepan. Stir in the evaporated milk and water.

Cook over medium heat until thickened, stirring constantly.

COMPANY'S COMING

Your guests are certain to request seconds when you serve them this delicious meal.

Warm Bleu Cheese, Bacon and Garlic Dip

SERVES 4 TO 6

7 slices bacon, chopped
2 garlic cloves, minced
8 ounces cream cheese, softened

1/4 cup half-and-half
4 ounces bleu cheese, crumbled
2 tablespoons chopped fresh chives

DIRECTIONS:

Preheat the oven to 350 degrees.

Cook the bacon in a skillet over medium heat until almost crisp; drain. Add the garlic. Cook until the bacon is crisp.

Beat the cream cheese in a mixing bowl until smooth. Add the half-and-half and mix well. Stir in the bacon mixture, bleu cheese and chives. Spoon into a 2-cup ovenproof serving dish and cover with foil.

Bake for 30 minutes or until heated through.

Serve with crackers.

Tomatoes with Mint Salsa

SERVES 4

1 large shallot, minced
   (about 2 tablespoons)
1/4 cup minced fresh mint
1 1/2 tablespoons balsamic vinegar
1 tablespoon sesame oil

2 1/2 tablespoons extra-virgin olive oil
1/4 teaspoon salt
freshly ground white pepper to taste
2 tomatoes, sliced

DIRECTIONS:

Combine the shallot, mint, vinegar, sesame oil, olive oil, salt and white pepper in a bowl and mix well. Let stand for 10 minutes.

Arrange the tomato slices in a serving dish. Pour the mint mixture over the tomatoes.

Serve at room temperature.

Menu

WARM BLEU CHEESE,
BACON AND GARLIC DIP

TOMATOES WITH
MINT SALSA

SAUTÉED SQUASH

GOURMET POTATOES

CASHEW AND ROSEMARY
ENCRUSTED SALMON
WITH LIME SAUCE

BAKED SEA BASS WITH
WALNUT BREAD CRUMB
CRUST AND
LEMON DILL SAUCE

STRAWBERRY
CHOCOLATE MERINGUE
TORTE

Sautéed Squash

2 tablespoons butter or margarine
1 tablespoon olive oil
2 yellow squash, coarsely grated
2 zucchini, coarsely grated

2 garlic cloves, minced
1 tablespoon snipped parsley
salt and pepper to taste

DIRECTIONS:

Heat the butter and olive oil in a skillet. Add the squash and zucchini.

Sauté for 5 minutes or until tender. Add the garlic, parsley, salt and pepper. Sauté for 2 minutes.

Serve immediately.

Gourmet Potatoes

6 medium potatoes
2 cups (8 ounces) shredded Cheddar cheese
1/4 cup (1/2 stick) butter
1 1/2 cups sour cream
1/3 cup chopped green onions

1 teaspoon salt
1/4 teaspoon pepper
2 tablespoons butter
paprika to taste

DIRECTIONS:

Cook the potatoes in water to cover in a saucepan until tender; drain and cool. Peel the potatoes and coarsely shred.

Preheat the oven to 350 degrees.

Melt the cheese and 1/4 cup butter in a saucepan over low heat, stirring constantly. Remove from the heat. Stir in the sour cream, green onions, salt and pepper. Fold in the potatoes. Spoon into a greased 2-quart baking dish. Dot with 2 tablespoons butter. Sprinkle with paprika.

Bake for 30 minutes.

Note: You may prepare ahead and bake when ready to serve.

Cashew and Rosemary Encrusted Salmon with Lime Sauce

SERVES 4

1/2 cup raw cashews, ground

1/3 cup shredded coconut

2 tablespoons chopped fresh rosemary

1/3 cup panko (Japanese bread crumbs)

1/2 cup flour

salt and pepper to taste

4 (6-ounce) salmon fillets, skinned

2 eggs, beaten

1/2 cup olive oil

2 tablespoons chopped shallots

1/4 cup white wine

1/2 cup heavy cream

1/2 cup (1 stick) butter, softened

juice of 2 limes

DIRECTIONS:

Mix the cashews, coconut, rosemary and panko in a shallow dish. Mix the flour, salt and pepper together. Dredge the fish in the flour mixture. Dip in the eggs. Roll in the cashew mixture.

Fry the fish in the hot olive oil in a skillet until the fish flakes easily. Remove the fish to a heated platter. Drain the skillet, reserving 1 tablespoon of the drippings.

Sauté the shallots in the reserved drippings until tender. Add the wine. Cook until almost all of the wine is absorbed. Add the cream. Cook until reduced by 1/2. Reduce the heat. Whisk in the butter and lime juice alternately until thoroughly incorporated. Adjust the seasonings to taste. Spoon over the fish.

To remove small pinbones from fish, turn a mixing bowl upside down and lay the fish across it flesh side up. The curve of the bowl will cause the bones to stick up so you can see and remove them more easily.

Baked Sea Bass with Walnut Bread Crumb Crust and Lemon Dill Sauce

SERVES 4

Cook fish perfectly by measuring it at its thickest part. Cook for 10 minutes per inch of thickness if grilling or sautéing, 15 minutes per inch if it's wrapped in foil or baked in a sauce.

4 (6-ounce) sea bass fillets
salt and pepper to taste
1 cup fresh French bread crumbs
3/4 cup walnuts
2 tablespoons unsalted butter, melted
2 tablespoons horseradish

1½ tablespoons Dijon mustard
1/4 cup finely grated Parmesan cheese
2 tablespoons minced fresh parsley
4 teaspoons olive oil
Lemon Dill Sauce (below)

DIRECTIONS:

Preheat the oven to 350 degrees.

Arrange the fish in a buttered 9×13-inch baking pan. Sprinkle with salt and pepper.

Process the bread crumbs and walnuts in a food processor until the walnuts are finely chopped. Combine with the butter, horseradish and Dijon mustard in a bowl. Stir in the cheese and parsley. Press the mixture gently onto the fish. Drizzle 1 teaspoon olive oil over each fillet.

Bake for 15 minutes or until the fish flakes easily.

Preheat the broiler.

Broil for 2 minutes or until the crust is golden brown, watching closely to prevent burning. Remove to serving plates. Serve with Lemon Dill Sauce.

Lemon Dill Sauce

3/4 cup dry white wine
3 tablespoons chopped shallots
2 tablespoons fresh lemon juice
1/2 cup (1 stick) unsalted butter,
    cut into 8 pieces

1½ tablespoons chopped fresh dill weed
salt and pepper to taste

DIRECTIONS:

Boil the wine, shallots and lemon juice in a medium saucepan over high heat for 6 minutes or until reduced to about 1/4 cup. Reduce the heat to low.

Whisk in the butter 1 piece at a time until melted. Remove from the heat. Stir in the dill weed. Season with salt and pepper.

Strawberry Chocolate Meringue Torte

SERVES 8

4 egg whites
1/4 teaspoon salt
1/4 teaspoon cream of tartar
1 cup sugar
2 cups sliced strawberries
1 teaspoon sugar

4 tablespoons semisweet chocolate chips
2 cups whipped topping

Garnish:
mint leaves

DIRECTIONS:

Preheat the oven to 250 degrees.

Cover a large baking sheet with parchment paper. Draw two 8-inch circles on the paper. Turn and secure with masking tape.

Beat the egg whites, salt and cream of tartar in a mixing bowl at high speed until foamy. Add 1 cup sugar 1 tablespoon at a time, beating until stiff peaks form. Spread 1/2 of the mixture into each circle on the prepared baking sheet using the back of a spoon.

Bake for 1 hour or until the meringues are crisp.

Sprinkle the strawberries with 1 teaspoon sugar in a bowl. Cover and set aside.

Sprinkle each meringue with 1 1/2 tablespoons chocolate chips. Return to the oven and turn off the heat. Let stand for 5 minutes. Spread the softened chocolate with a spatula. Cool to room temperature.

Arrange 1 meringue on a serving platter. Spread 1 cup whipped topping over the top. Spoon 1/2 of the strawberry mixture over the whipped topping. Top with the remaining meringue. Repeat layers with the remaining whipped topping and strawberry mixture.

Place the remaining 1 tablespoon chocolate chips in a small microwave-safe bowl. Microwave on High for 1 minute or until the chocolate chips are soft. Stir the chocolate and drizzle over the torte. Garnish with mint leaves.

PHOTOGRAPH ON PAGE 44

BRIDESMAIDS' LUNCHEON

Weddings—and all the preparations that go into planning them—are a time of excitement and joy. Honor the bride and her closest friends with this menu.

Lime Mint Tea

MAKES 10 CUPS

4 cups water
6 regular-size tea bags
2 cups loosely packed fresh mint leaves, chopped
4 1/2 cups water

1 1/2 cups sugar
1 1/4 cups lemon juice
1/3 cup fresh lime juice

Garnish:
fresh mint

DIRECTIONS:

Bring 4 cups water to a boil in a saucepan. Pour over the tea bags in a bowl. Steep for 5 minutes; discard the tea bags. Stir in the mint. Let stand for 15 minutes. Pour through a wire-mesh strainer into a bowl, discarding the mint.

Bring 4 1/2 cups water and the sugar to a boil in a saucepan. Remove from the heat to cool. Stir in the tea, lemon juice and lime juice. Pour into a large pitcher. Chill, covered, in the refrigerator. Serve over ice and garnish with fresh mint.

Spinach Pesto Pie

SERVES 16

1 1/2 cups reduced-fat cottage cheese
1 (10-ounce) package frozen chopped spinach, thawed
8 ounces reduced-fat cream cheese
1/4 cup grated Parmesan cheese

1 egg
2 egg whites
2 garlic cloves, minced
2 teaspoons basil
1/4 teaspoon salt
1/8 teaspoon pepper

DIRECTIONS:

Preheat the oven to 325 degrees.

Press the liquid from the cottage cheese and spinach. Process the cottage cheese, spinach, cream cheese, Parmesan cheese, egg, egg whites, garlic, basil, salt and pepper in a food processor until smooth. Pour into a 9-inch springform pan sprayed with nonstick cooking spray.

Bake for 1 hour or until firm. Cool slightly before cutting to serve.

PHOTOGRAPH LEFT: STRAWBERRY CHOCOLATE MERINGUE TORTE

Menu

LIME MINT TEA

SPINACH PESTO PIE

COLD RASPBERRY SOUP

COLD TWO-MELON SOUP

CHICKEN AND ARTICHOKE SALAD

PASTA WITH PROSCIUTTO, PEPPERS AND HERBS

POPPY SEED BREAD

LEMON CHEESE BITES

BERRY AND GINGER SOUR CREAM BRÛLÉE

Cold Raspberry Soup

When making flavored tea or punch with mint, freeze chopped mint leaves with water in ice cube trays to make flavored cubes.

SERVES 6

2 (10-ounce) packages frozen raspberries, thawed
1/2 cup sour cream

1/3 cup sugar
2 cups water
1/2 cup dry red wine

DIRECTIONS:

Purée the raspberries in a blender. Add the sour cream and sugar and process until smooth. Stir in the water and wine. Spoon into an airtight container.

Chill, covered, for 8 to 12 hours. Shake or stir well before serving. Serve cold.

Cold Two-Melon Soup

SERVES 8

3 cups coarsely chopped cantaloupe
3 cups coarsely chopped honeydew melon
1/3 cup fresh lime juice
2 cups fresh orange juice

1/4 cup honey
2 cups dry Champagne
1 cup whipping cream, whipped
8 strawberries

DIRECTIONS:

Chop 1/2 of the cantaloupe and 1/2 of the honeydew melon finely.

Combine the remaining cantaloupe, honeydew melon, lime juice, orange juice and honey in a blender and process for several seconds. Pour into a large bowl. Stir in the finely chopped cantaloupe, honeydew melon and Champagne.

Chill, covered, until ready to serve.

Pour into soup bowls. Top with the whipped cream and strawberries.

Chicken and Artichoke Salad

6 chicken breasts, cooked and chopped
1 cup salad olives, drained
2 (14-ounce) cans artichoke hearts, drained and sliced
1 medium red onion, sliced
1/4 large green bell pepper, chopped
1/2 cup chopped celery
8 ounces fresh mushrooms, sliced
1/2 cup black olives, sliced
1/4 cup vegetable oil
1/4 cup olive oil
1/4 cup balsamic vinegar
1 tablespoon lemon juice
salt, black pepper and cayenne pepper to taste

DIRECTIONS:

Combine the chicken, salad olives, artichoke hearts, onion, bell pepper, celery, mushrooms and black olives in a large bowl and toss to mix well.

Whisk the vegetable oil, olive oil, vinegar, lemon juice, salt, black pepper and cayenne pepper in a small bowl until blended. Pour over the chicken mixture and toss to coat.

Chill, covered, for 8 to 10 hours. Serve over curly lettuce leaves.

Pasta with Prosciutto, Peppers and Herbs

16 ounces campanelle or rotini
1 red onion, finely chopped
2 yellow bell peppers, finely chopped
2 tablespoons olive oil
1 (13-ounce) jar roasted red peppers, drained and finely chopped
6 ounces prosciutto or ham, finely chopped (about 1 1/2 cups)
1/4 cup olive oil
2 cups lightly packed mixed fresh herbs,
*   such as basil and parsley, finely chopped*
salt and pepper to taste

Garnish:
freshly grated Parmesan cheese

DIRECTIONS:

Cook the pasta using the package directions until al dente; drain well.

Sauté the onion and bell peppers in 2 tablespoons olive oil in a skillet over medium-low heat until softened. Stir in the red peppers and prosciutto.

Combine the pasta, prosciutto mixture, 1/4 cup olive oil, herbs, salt and pepper in a large bowl and toss to mix well. Garnish with cheese.

Poppy Seed Bread

⟡

To test the freshness of an egg, place it in a bowl of cold water. If the egg floats, don't use it.

3 cups flour
1¹/2 teaspoons salt
1¹/2 teaspoons baking powder
3 eggs
1 cup plus 2 tablespoons vegetable oil
2¹/2 cups sugar

1¹/2 cups milk
1¹/2 tablespoons poppy seeds
1¹/2 teaspoons vanilla extract
1¹/2 teaspoons almond extract
1¹/2 teaspoons butter flavoring
Confectioners' Sugar Glaze (below)

DIRECTIONS:

Preheat the oven to 350 degrees.

Mix the flour, salt and baking powder together. Beat the eggs, oil and sugar in a mixing bowl until blended. Add the flour mixture alternately with the milk, beating well after each addition. Stir in the poppy seeds and flavorings. (The batter will be thin.) Pour into 4 greased and floured 4×7-inch loaf pans.

Bake for 45 to 50 minutes or until a wooden pick inserted in the centers come out clean. Remove from the oven. Punch holes in the tops of the hot loaves with a wooden pick. Pour Confectioners' Sugar Glaze over the tops. Let stand for 20 minutes. Remove from the pans to cool.

Note: You may bake in 2 greased and floured 5×7-inch loaf pans and increase the baking time.

Confectioners' Sugar Glaze

3/4 cup confectioners' sugar
1/2 teaspoon lemon juice
1/2 teaspoon vanilla extract

1/2 teaspoon almond extract
1/2 teaspoon butter flavoring
orange juice

DIRECTIONS:

Combine the confectioners' sugar, lemon juice and flavorings in a bowl and mix until smooth. Stir in enough orange juice to make of a glaze consistency.

Lemon Cheese Bites

SERVES 10 TO 12

16 ounces cream cheese, softened
3/4 cup sugar
2 eggs
1 tablespoon lemon juice

1 teaspoon vanilla extract
vanilla wafers
chopped nuts or fruit (optional)

DIRECTIONS:

Preheat the oven to 350 degrees.

Beat the cream cheese and sugar in a mixing bowl until light and fluffy. Add the eggs, lemon juice and vanilla and mix well.

Place a vanilla wafer in each paper-lined muffin cup. Drop a spoonful of the cream cheese mixture into the prepared cups. Top each with nuts or fruit.

Bake for 15 minutes. Chill, covered, until ready to serve.

Don't be afraid to set an eclectic table. Experiment with various textures and patterns, but be sure to tie the theme together through color or shape. Mixing and matching china and crystal can also make an interesting and fun table.

Berry and Ginger Sour Cream Brûlée

SERVES 6

3 cups mixed fruit, such as blueberries, raspberries, strawberry halves and seedless grapes
1 1/2 cups sour cream

1 tablespoon finely chopped candied ginger
1 1/2 teaspoons vanilla extract
3 tablespoons light brown sugar

DIRECTIONS:

Preheat the broiler.

Arrange the fruit in a single layer in a small gratin or other shallow flame-proof dish.

Combine the sour cream, ginger and vanilla in a small bowl and mix well. Dollop over the fruit and spread to cover the fruit completely. Rub the brown sugar through a sieve evenly over the top.

Broil 3 inches from the heat source for 2 minutes or until the brown sugar is melted. Serve immediately.

Summer

❧

VEGETABLES ARE A MUST ON A DIET. I SUGGEST CARROT
CAKE, ZUCCHINI BREAD, AND PUMPKIN PIE.

—Garfield, in a comic strip by Jim Davis

Summer is a time to relax with friends in the warm outdoors. We watch beautiful sunsets and feel the fragrant breeze as it brushes our skin. We take trips to the local farmer's market and savor the fresh, perfectly ripe fruits and vegetables.

Any one of the following menus will help you enjoy the beautiful summer weather. Grill at the Dad's Cookout. Congratulate friends at the Engagement Cocktail Party. Pack a picnic to celebrate the Fourth of July. Share laughs and hugs at the Family Reunion. Whatever you do, just relax and enjoy the beautiful summer season.

Celebrate Dad on Father's Day with this casual yet delicious menu. If Dad likes to cook, let him do the grilling; or give him the day off so he can simply enjoy the day.

Spicy Black Bean Dip

SERVES 6 TO 8

2 (15-ounce) cans black beans, rinsed and drained
1/2 cup chopped onion
2 garlic cloves, minced
1/4 cup olive oil
1 (10-ounce) can tomatoes with green chiles
1/3 cup picante sauce
1/2 teaspoon cumin

1/2 teaspoon chili powder
1/4 cup shredded Monterey Jack cheese
1/4 cup chopped fresh cilantro
1 tablespoon fresh lime juice

Garnishes:
lime slices
chopped fresh cilantro

DIRECTIONS:

Mash the black beans in a bowl lightly. Sauté the onion and garlic in the olive oil in a skillet. Add the black beans and tomatoes with green chiles. Stir in the picante sauce, cumin and chili powder.

Cook until heated through. Stir in the cheese, 1/4 cup cilantro and lime juice. Spoon into a serving bowl. Garnish with lime slices and chopped cilantro. Serve hot with tortilla chips.

Mango Spinach Salad with Citrus Chipotle Vinaigrette

SERVES 4 TO 6

1 red bell pepper, roasted
1 green bell pepper, roasted
1 cup cubed fresh mango
1 cup cubed fresh pineapple
1 cup julienned peeled jicama

1/2 cup julienned carrots
1/2 cup Citrus Chipotle Vinaigrette
   (below)
8 ounces fresh spinach, trimmed
Pickled Onion Rings (page 54)

DIRECTIONS:

Combine the roasted bell peppers, mango, pineapple, jicama and carrots in a bowl and toss to mix. Add the Citrus Chipotle Vinaigrette and toss to coat.

Serve over the spinach and top with Pickled Onion Rings.

Note: You may add four 4-ounce boneless skinless chicken breasts, smoked and cut into bite-size pieces.

Citrus Chipotle Vinaigrette

MAKES ABOUT 3/4 CUP

1/4 cup frozen orange juice concentrate,
   thawed
2 tablespoons frozen orange tangerine
   juice concentrate, thawed
juice of 1 lime
1 tablespoon water

2 tablespoons olive oil
1 teaspoon minced garlic
1 teaspoon Dijon mustard
1 1/2 tablespoons minced fresh basil
2 teaspoons adobo paste

DIRECTIONS:

Whisk the orange juice concentrate, orange tangerine juice concentrate, lime juice, water, olive oil, garlic, Dijon mustard, basil and adobo paste in a bowl until smooth.

Chill, covered, in the refrigerator until ready to serve.

Pickled Onion Rings

When smoking wood chips for your grill, add wine, broth, or fresh herbs to the water pan for even more flavor.

MAKES 1/2 CUP

1/2 cup red onion rings
1/2 cup herbal or red wine vinegar

1/2 cup water

DIRECTIONS:

Arrange the onion rings in a glass bowl.

Bring the vinegar and water to a boil in a small saucepan. Pour over the onion rings.

Let stand for 30 minutes or longer.

Grilled Vegetable Medley

SERVES 4 TO 6

1 cup thickly sliced zucchini
1 cup thickly sliced yellow squash
1 red bell pepper, cut into 1/2-inch strips
1 green bell pepper, cut into 1/2-inch strips
1 medium yellow onion, cut into wedges
3 portobello mushroom caps, cut into 1/2-inch strips

1/3 cup extra-virgin olive oil
1/4 cup balsamic vinegar
1/3 cup chopped fresh basil leaves
1/2 teaspoon garlic powder
dash of salt and pepper

DIRECTIONS:

Preheat the grill.

Combine the zucchini, yellow squash, bell peppers, onion, and portobello mushrooms in a large bowl and toss to mix. Whisk the olive oil, vinegar, basil, garlic powder, salt and pepper in a small bowl until smooth. Pour over the vegetables and toss to coat. Place in a foil roasting bag. Place on a grill rack on the top shelf.

Grill for 20 to 25 minutes or until the vegetables are tender. Punch holes in the bag after grilling to allow the steam to escape.

Note: You may also bake in a preheated 425-degree oven for 25 minutes.

Parslied New Potatoes

Serves 6

Brush your grill with vegetable oil to prevent meat from sticking.

1¹/2 pounds small red potatoes
1 tablespoon vegetable oil
1 medium onion, chopped
1 small garlic clove, crushed

1 cup chicken broth
³/4 cup chopped fresh parsley
¹/2 teaspoon pepper
¹/4 cup chopped fresh parsley

DIRECTIONS:

Peel a strip from around the middle of each potato. Place in a pan and cover with cold water. Set aside.

Heat a large skillet over medium-high heat. Add the oil, onion and garlic. Sauté for 5 minutes or until tender. Add the broth and ³/4 cup parsley and mix well.

Bring to a boil. Arrange the potatoes in a single layer in the skillet. Return to a boil and reduce the heat. Simmer, covered, for 10 minutes or until the potatoes are tender. Remove with a slotted spoon to a serving bowl, reserving the sauce in the skillet.

Add the pepper to the reserved sauce and stir to mix. Pour over the potatoes. Sprinkle with ¹/4 cup parsley.

Grilled Marinated Pot Roast

Serves 4 to 6

1 (3-pound) chuck roast
unseasoned meat tenderizer (optional)
1 (8-ounce) bottle soy sauce, or more
    to taste
¹/4 cup packed brown sugar

¹/4 cup bourbon
1 teaspoon lemon juice
1 teaspoon Worcestershire sauce
¹/2 cup water

DIRECTIONS:

Sprinkle the beef with meat tenderizer and pierce with a fork. Place in a sealable plastic bag.

Mix the soy sauce, brown sugar, bourbon, lemon juice, Worcestershire sauce and water in a bowl. Pour over the beef and seal the bag.

Marinate in the refrigerator for 3 hours or longer, turning occasionally. Preheat the grill.

Drain the beef, discarding the marinade. Place on a grill rack.

Grill over medium-high heat for 60 to 70 minutes or to the desired degree of doneness.

Marinated Pork Loin

1 (4- to 5-pound) pork tenderloin
2 tablespoons dry mustard
2 teaspoons thyme
1/2 cup dry sherry
1/2 cup soy sauce
1/4 teaspoon garlic powder, or
   2 garlic cloves, minced

1 teaspoon ground ginger
1 (10-ounce) jar orange preserves or
   apricot preserves
2 tablespoons soy sauce
2 tablespoons dry sherry

DIRECTIONS:

Place the pork in a sealable plastic bag. Mix the dry mustard, thyme, sherry, soy sauce, garlic powder and ginger in a bowl. Pour over the pork and seal the bag. Marinate in the refrigerator for 8 to 12 hours.

Preheat the grill. Drain the pork, discarding the marinade. Place the pork on a grill rack. Grill over indirect heat with the grill lid down for 50 to 55 minutes or until a meat thermometer inserted into the thick portion registers 170 degrees.

Mix the preserves, soy sauce and sherry in a saucepan. Brush some of the sauce over the pork to glaze. Remove the pork to a serving platter. Heat the remaining sauce and serve with the pork.

Raspberry Cream Pie

1 cup sugar
1/3 cup flour
2 eggs, lightly beaten
1 1/3 cups sour cream
1 teaspoon vanilla extract
3 cups fresh raspberries or thawed
   frozen raspberries
1 unbaked (9-inch) pie shell

1/3 cup flour
1/3 cup packed brown sugar
1/3 cup chopped pecans
3 tablespoons butter, softened

Garnishes:
whipped cream
fresh raspberries

DIRECTIONS:

Preheat the oven to 400 degrees.

Combine the sugar, 1/3 cup flour, eggs, sour cream and vanilla in a large bowl and mix well. Fold in 3 cups raspberries gradually. Spoon into the pie shell. Bake for 30 to 35 minutes or until the center is set.

Mix 1/3 cup flour, the brown sugar, pecans and butter in a small bowl. Sprinkle over the hot pie. Bake for 10 minutes or until golden brown. Cool on a wire rack. Garnish with whipped cream and fresh raspberries.

MEXICAN FIESTA

Throw a fiesta with this mouthwatering menu that includes a fabulous combination of Interior Mexican and Tex-Mex flavors.

Margaritas by the Gallon

SERVES 20

1 (12-ounce) can frozen lemonade
    concentrate, thawed
1 (6-ounce) can frozen limeade
    concentrate, thawed

2 cups lime juice
1 cup Rose's lime juice
1 fifth tequila
12 ounces Triple Sec

DIRECTIONS:

Combine the lemonade concentrate, limeade concentrate, lime juice, tequila and Triple Sec in a 1-gallon jug. Add enough water to fill and mix well.

Chill, covered, in the refrigerator until ready to serve.

Fiesta Guacamole

SERVES 6 TO 8

2 medium avocados
1 small tomato, finely chopped
2 tablespoons minced onion
1 teaspoon lime juice

1/2 teaspoon garlic powder
1/2 teaspoon salt
2 tablespoons cilantro leaves

DIRECTIONS:

Mash the avocados with a fork in a medium bowl. Stir in the tomato, onion, lime juice, garlic powder, salt and cilantro.

Spoon into a serving bowl. Serve with tortilla chips.

Note: If you are not planning to serve immediately, place the avocado seeds in the guacamole and chill, covered, until ready to serve.

Mexican Salad Bowl

2 quarts bite-size crisp salad greens
1/4 cup shredded Cheddar cheese
1/4 cup chopped green onions
1/4 cup sliced pitted black olives

2 medium tomatoes, cut into 8 wedges
    each
1 cup coarsely crushed corn chips
Avocado Dressing (below)

DIRECTIONS:

Combine the salad greens, cheese, green onions and olives in a salad bowl and
toss to mix.

Add the tomato wedges. Sprinkle with the corn chips. Add Avocado
Dressing and toss lightly.

Avocado Dressing

1 small ripe avocado (8 ounces)
2 tablespoons lemon juice
1/2 cup sour cream
1/4 cup vegetable oil

1/2 teaspoon sugar
1 teaspoon seasoned salt
1/2 teaspoon chili powder

DIRECTIONS:

Cut the avocado into halves lengthwise. Remove the pit and peel. Mash the
avocado and lemon juice in a medium bowl until chunky. Add the sour cream,
oil, sugar, seasoned salt and chili powder and mix well.

Chill, covered with plastic wrap, for several hours.

Jalapeño Spinach

For a casual outdoor party, decorate with colorful candles placed on Mexican tiles.

4 (10-ounce) packages frozen chopped
   spinach
1/2 cup (1 stick) butter
1 small onion, chopped
1/4 cup flour
1 cup evaporated milk
2 teaspoons Worcestershire sauce

2 teaspoons lemon juice
1 teaspoon salt
1 teaspoon black pepper
dash of cayenne pepper
2 (6-ounce) rolls jalapeño cheese
bread crumbs for topping

DIRECTIONS:

Preheat the oven to 350 degrees.

Cook the spinach using the package directions. Drain, reserving 1 cup of the liquid.

Melt the butter in a large skillet. Add the onion. Sauté until tender. Add the flour and mix until smooth. Add the evaporated milk and reserved liquid gradually, stirring constantly.

Cook over medium heat until thickened, stirring constantly. Add the Worcestershire sauce, lemon juice, salt, black pepper, cayenne pepper and cheese. Cook until the cheese is melted, stirring constantly. Add the spinach and mix well. Spoon into a 9×13-inch baking pan. Sprinkle with bread crumbs.

Bake for 45 minutes or until bubbly.

Note: Make the day before to allow the flavors to blend. This recipe freezes well.

Enchiladas de Res

1 pound lean ground beef
3/4 cup chopped onion
1 garlic clove, minced
1 small zucchini, finely chopped
1 small carrot, finely chopped
3/4 cup finely chopped peeled potato
reduced-sodium beef stock
2 tomatoes, peeled, seeded and puréed
1 tablespoon parsley
1/4 teaspoon cinnamon
1/8 teaspoon ground cloves
2 cups reduced-sodium beef stock

12 corn tortillas
1/2 cup canned tomato purée
3 tablespoons chili powder
2 teaspoons cumin
1/2 teaspoon garlic powder
shredded lettuce
thinly sliced radishes
minced onion
sliced pickled jalapeño chiles
vinegar
olive oil

DIRECTIONS:

Preheat the oven to 400 degrees.

Brown the ground beef, 3/4 cup onion and the garlic in a skillet until the ground beef is crumbly. Add the zucchini, carrot and potato. Add enough beef stock to cover.

Simmer until the vegetables are tender. Drain, reserving 2 cups of the liquid.

Return the ground beef mixture to the skillet. Add the tomatoes, parsley, cinnamon, cloves and 2 cups beef stock. Cook until almost all of the liquid has evaporated.

Steam the tortillas briefly to soften. Fill with the ground beef mixture and roll up. Arrange in a baking dish.

Simmer the reserved liquid, tomato purée, chili powder, cumin and garlic powder in a saucepan over medium heat until reduced to a sauce consistency. Pour over the enchiladas.

Bake for 15 minutes or until heated through. Toss lettuce, radishes, minced onion and jalapeño chiles with a little vinegar and olive oil in a bowl. Spoon over the top of the enchiladas.

Lime-Grilled Chicken with Black Bean Sauce

For a green garnish alternative to parsley, use carrot tops, peppergrass sprouts, fresh bay leaves, or little bundles of fresh herbs like cilantro or basil.

SERVES 4

4 (4-ounce) boneless skinless chicken breasts
2 tablespoons fresh lime juice
1 tablespoon vegetable oil
1/4 teaspoon cayenne pepper
4 garlic cloves, minced

Black Bean Sauce (below)

Garnishes:
1/2 cup chopped red bell pepper
1 tablespoon chopped purple onion
fresh cilantro

DIRECTIONS:

Place the chicken in a sealable plastic bag. Mix the lime juice, oil, cayenne pepper and garlic in a bowl. Pour over the chicken and seal the bag.

Marinate in the refrigerator for 8 hours, turning occasionally.

Preheat the grill.

Drain the chicken, discarding the marinade. Arrange the chicken on a grill rack.

Grill until the chicken is cooked through.

To serve, spoon Black Bean Sauce onto each serving plate and top with a piece of chicken. Garnish with red bell pepper, purple onion and cilantro.

Black Bean Sauce

1 cup drained cooked black beans
1/2 cup orange juice
2 tablespoons balsamic vinegar

1/4 teaspoon salt
1/8 teaspoon freshly ground pepper
2 garlic cloves, minced

DIRECTIONS:

Blend the black beans, orange juice, vinegar, salt, pepper and garlic in a food processor. Pour into a small saucepan.

Simmer until heated through.

PHOTOGRAPH ON PAGE 62

Lace Cookies

MAKES ABOUT 2 DOZEN

1/2 cup flour
1/4 teaspoon baking powder
1/2 cup sugar
1/2 cup old-fashioned rolled oats
1 tablespoon grated orange zest

1/2 cup toasted pecans, chopped
2 tablespoons heavy cream
6 tablespoons unsalted butter, melted
2 tablespoons light corn syrup

DIRECTIONS:

Preheat the oven to 325 degrees.

Mix the flour, baking powder, sugar, oats, orange zest and pecans in a large bowl. Stir in the cream, butter and corn syrup. Drop by teaspoonfuls 2 inches apart onto cookie sheets lined with parchment paper.

Bake for 8 minutes. Remove from the oven and let stand until cool enough to handle. Remove the hot cookies with a spatula and quickly drape over a lightly buttered rolling pin. Let stand until cool. Slide off the rolling pin and store in an airtight container.

Pralines

MAKES ABOUT 2 POUNDS

2 cups sugar
1 cup buttermilk
1 teaspoon baking soda

3/4 cup (1 1/2 sticks) butter
1 teaspoon vanilla extract
2 cups chopped pecans

DIRECTIONS:

Combine the sugar, buttermilk, baking soda and butter in a large saucepan. Cook to 234 to 240 degrees on a candy thermometer, soft-ball stage, stirring to scrape the bottom of the pan frequently. Remove from the heat. Beat by hand until the mixture darkens in color. Add the vanilla and pecans. Beat until the mixture is thick enough to drop onto waxed paper. (Place the pan in hot water to soften if the mixture becomes too hard.)

Drop by spoonfuls onto waxed paper.

PHOTOGRAPH LEFT:
LIME-GRILLED CHICKEN WITH BLACK BEAN SAUCE

Orange Caramel Flan

For a casual decoration that smells wonderful, place freshly cut sprigs of rosemary in bud vases.

1/2 cup sugar
1/4 cup water
2 cups milk
1 (1-inch) cinnamon stick
peel of 1 orange
3 eggs

2 egg yolks
1/2 cup sugar
1 teaspoon orange liqueur

Garnish:
fresh orange slices

DIRECTIONS:

Preheat the oven to 350 degrees.

Bring 1/2 cup sugar and the water to a boil in a saucepan. Boil until the mixture is dark and amber in color; do not stir. Pour into 6 ovenproof custard cups. Let stand until cool.

Bring the milk, cinnamon stick and orange peel to a boil gradually in a saucepan. Remove from the heat. Let stand for 10 minutes or until cool. Strain into a bowl, discarding the cinnamon stick and orange peel.

Beat the eggs, egg yolks, 1/2 cup sugar and liqueur in a bowl until blended. Whisk into the milk mixture. Strain into a bowl. Spoon into the prepared custard cups. Cover with foil.

Place the custard cups in a large baking pan. Add enough hot water to the baking pan to come halfway up the sides of the custard cups.

Bake for 30 minutes or until set. Remove to wire racks to cool.

To serve, unmold onto individual dessert plates, allowing the caramel to run over the top. Garnish with orange slices.

POOL PARTY

Take advantage of the beautiful summer weather by treating your friends to a day or evening by the pool. You will find this tropical menu both festive and tasty.

Piña Colada Slush

MAKES 6 QUARTS

1 (46-ounce) can pineapple juice
2 (12-ounce) cans frozen lemonade
   concentrate, thawed
3 cups water

2 cups light rum
1 (15-ounce) can cream of coconut
1 (3-liter) bottle lemon-lime soda, chilled

DIRECTIONS:

Combine the pineapple juice, lemonade concentrate, water, rum and cream of coconut in a large plastic container and mix well.

Freeze for 8 hours or longer, stirring twice.

To serve, combine equal portions of the frozen mixture and lemon-lime soda in a pitcher and mix well. Store any remaining frozen mixture in the freezer.

Tomato, Basil and Mozzarella Skewers

SERVES 12 TO 15

1/2 cup olive oil
1/4 cup balsamic vinegar
1 garlic clove, crushed
salt and pepper to taste

1 pint cherry tomatoes
small to medium basil leaves
8 ounces mozzarella cheese, cut into cubes

DIRECTIONS:

Whisk the olive oil, vinegar and garlic in a bowl until emulsified. Season with salt and pepper.

To assemble, alternate the tomatoes with basil leaves and cheese cubes on skewers, leaving plenty of room at the bottom to pick up the skewers.

Marinate in the vinaigrette for 30 minutes. Serve at room temperature for the best flavor.

PHOTOGRAPH ON PAGE 86

Menu

PIÑA COLADA SLUSH

▪▪

TOMATO, BASIL AND
MOZZARELLA SKEWERS

▪▪

CHILLED CARROT SOUP
WITH CUMIN AND LIME

▪▪

CALYPSO SALAD

▪▪

JACK DANIEL'S SALMON

▪▪

GRILLED FLANK
STEAK WITH
PROVENÇAL SPICES

▪▪

LEMON RIPPLE
ICE CREAM PIE

▪▪

TROPICAL FRUIT
KABOBS WITH
CARAMEL SAUCE

Chilled Carrot Soup with Cumin and Lime

2 tablespoons olive oil
2 pounds carrots, chopped
white and pale green portions of 2 leeks,
    chopped
1 tablespoon minced garlic
3 1/2 teaspoons cumin
1/2 teaspoon crushed red pepper
6 1/2 cups canned reduced-sodium
    chicken broth

6 tablespoons sour cream
2 tablespoons fresh lime juice
salt and black pepper to taste
2 tablespoons sour cream
2 tablespoons chopped fresh cilantro
2 teaspoons lime zest

DIRECTIONS:

Heat the olive oil in a large heavy saucepan over medium-high heat. Add the carrots and leeks. Sauté for 5 minutes or until the leeks begin to soften but not brown. Add the garlic; sauté for 1 minute. Add the cumin and red pepper. Sauté for 30 seconds longer. Add the broth. Bring to a boil and reduce the heat. Simmer, uncovered, for 35 minutes or until the vegetables are tender.

Purée the soup in batches in a blender until smooth. Pour into a large bowl. Whisk in 6 tablespoons sour cream. Chill, covered, for 4 to 12 hours.

To serve, stir the lime juice into the soup. Season with salt and black pepper. Ladle into 4 soup bowls. Top each with 1 1/2 teaspoons sour cream. Sprinkle with cilantro and lime zest.

Calypso Salad

SERVES 24

Julienne the green top of scallions to create a pretty, frilly garnish.

2²/3 cups water
1¹/3 cups long grain rice
2 teaspoons salt
4 teaspoons olive oil
2 cups chopped onions
2 cups chopped red bell peppers
4 cups chopped tomatoes

1 cup chopped fresh cilantro
4 (15-ounce) cans black beans, rinsed
    and drained
1/4 cup red wine vinegar
1/4 cup fresh lime juice
1/2 cup olive oil
4 avocados, sliced or chopped

DIRECTIONS:

Bring the water to a boil in a saucepan. Stir in the rice, salt and 4 teaspoons olive oil. Reduce the heat to low. Cook, covered, for 20 minutes or until the rice is tender and the water is absorbed. Rinse with cold water and drain.

Combine the rice, onions, bell peppers, tomatoes, cilantro and black beans in a bowl and mix well. Whisk the vinegar, lime juice and 1/2 cup olive oil in a bowl until emulsified. Stir into the black bean mixture.

Chill, covered, for 3 to 12 hours. Top with the avocados and serve.

Jack Daniel's Salmon

SERVES 3 TO 4

1¹/2 pounds salmon fillets or steaks
1/4 cup Jack Daniel's whiskey
1/4 cup orange juice
3 tablespoons soy sauce

2 tablespoons olive oil
2 tablespoons chopped fresh parsley
1 garlic clove, minced
1 teaspoon basil

DIRECTIONS:

Arrange the fish in a single layer in a shallow dish. Mix the whiskey, orange juice, soy sauce, olive oil, parsley and garlic in a bowl. Pour over the fish.

Marinate at room temperature for 1 hour or in the refrigerator for 6 hours. Preheat the grill.

Drain the fish, reserving the marinade. Arrange the fish on a grill rack. Brush with some of the reserved marinade.

Grill until the fish flakes easily, turning and basting with the remaining reserved marinade.

Grilled Flank Steak with Provençal Spices

—

SERVES 4

3 tablespoons extra-virgin olive oil
1 teaspoon salt
2 garlic cloves, peeled
2 teaspoons fresh rosemary leaves
2 teaspoons fresh lavender leaves, or
   1/2 teaspoon dried lavender

2 teaspoons fennel seeds
2 teaspoons fresh thyme leaves
1 teaspoon cracked pepper
1 1/2 to 2 pounds flank steak

DIRECTIONS:

Preheat the grill.

Process the olive oil, salt, garlic, rosemary, lavender, fennel seeds, thyme and pepper in a food processor until the herbs are minced; do not purée. Rub over the steak. Arrange the steak on a grill rack.

Grill for 4 minutes on each side or until brown for medium-rare, turning once. Remove from the heat. Let stand for 5 minutes before thinly slicing.

For a casual outdoor event, decorate with pillar candles wrapped in fresh asparagus or green beans. Place a rubber band around a tall pillar candle and slide the vegetables between the rubber band and candle. Add the vegetables until the candle is completely surrounded. Tie a piece of thin rope around the candle and over the rubber band. This idea can also be used with cinnamon sticks and ribbon in the winter.

Lemon Ripple Ice Cream Pie

—

SERVES 10 TO 12

1/2 gallon vanilla ice cream, softened
   slightly
Graham Cracker Crust (page 69)
Lemon Curd (page 69)

Garnish:
toasted almonds

DIRECTIONS:

Spread 1/2 of the ice cream in the Graham Cracker Crust. Spoon 1/2 of the Lemon Curd over the ice cream. Spoon the remaining ice cream over the Lemon Curd. Spoon the remaining Lemon Curd by tablespoonfuls over the ice cream. Swirl the Lemon Curd into the ice cream with a small knife to form an attractive design.

Freeze for 1 hour or until firm. Cover with plastic wrap. Freeze for 8 to 12 hours. (You may prepare 2 days ahead.)

To serve, let the pie stand at room temperature for 10 minutes. Remove the side of the pan. Cut into wedges and arrange on serving plates. Garnish with toasted almonds.

Lemon Curd

1 cup sugar
6 tablespoons unsalted butter,
   cut into small pieces
1/3 cup fresh lemon juice

2 eggs
2 egg yolks
1 teaspoon lemon zest

DIRECTIONS:

Combine the sugar, butter and lemon juice in a double boiler. Heat over simmering water until the sugar dissolves and the butter melts. Beat the eggs, egg yolks and lemon zest in a bowl until blended. Whisk the warm mixture gradually into the egg mixture. Return to the double boiler.

Cook over simmering water for 10 minutes or until the mixture thickens and leaves a path on the back of a spoon when the finger is drawn across, stirring constantly; do not boil. Spoon into a bowl and whisk until smooth if needed. Cover with plastic wrap, pressing directly onto the surface.

Chill for 1 hour or longer. (You may prepare up to 3 days ahead.)

Graham Cracker Crust

1¼ cups ground toasted almonds
   (about 5 ounces)
1 cup graham cracker crumbs
   (5 whole graham crackers)

7 tablespoons unsalted butter, melted
2 teaspoons lemon zest
1/2 teaspoon almond extract

DIRECTIONS:

Preheat the oven to 325 degrees.

Mix the almonds, graham cracker crumbs, butter, lemon zest and almond extract in a medium bowl until the mixture is evenly moistened. Press over the bottom and 1 inch up the side of a buttered 9-inch springform pan.

Bake for 8 minutes. Cool on a wire rack.

Tropical Fruit Kabobs with Caramel Sauce

To save time the day of your party, set your table the night before but be sure to turn your glasses or stemware upside down to keep dust out.

SERVES 6

1 large mango, peeled and cubed
1/2 papaya, peeled and cubed
1/4 cup lime juice
2 tablespoons dark rum
2 teaspoons vanilla extract
1 cup semisweet white wine

1/4 cup packed brown sugar
6 whole cloves
1 cinnamon stick
1 medium pineapple, cored and cubed
1 orange, cut into 1/2-inch wedges

DIRECTIONS:

Process 1 cup of the mango and papaya cubes with the lime juice, rum and vanilla in a food processor until smooth.

Combine the wine, brown sugar, cloves and cinnamon stick in a medium saucepan and mix well. Cook over medium heat for 12 to 15 minutes. Cook over medium-high heat for 10 minutes; do not stir. Remove from the heat. Let stand for 1 minute. Discard the cloves and cinnamon stick. Stir in the mango and papaya mixture gradually.

Preheat the grill.

Thread the remaining mango and papaya cubes, pineapple and orange wedges alternately on 6 skewers. Arrange on a grill rack.

Grill for 8 minutes or until light brown, basting occasionally with some of the sauce. Serve with the remaining sauce.

FOURTH OF JULY PICNIC

Celebrate Independence Day with this patriotic American fare. The colors are appealing while the flavors will make your taste buds "sparkle" with delight.

Roasted Pepper Pesto Dip

SERVES 10 TO 12

16 ounces cream cheese, softened
8 ounces (or more) goat cheese
1/2 cup whipping cream

7 ounces prepared pesto
1 (12-ounce) jar roasted red bell peppers, cut into 1-inch strips

DIRECTIONS:

Beat the cream cheese, goat cheese and whipping cream in a mixing bowl until smooth.

Reserve a small amount of the pesto for the top. Reserve several bell pepper strips for garnish. Spread 1/3 of the cream cheese mixture in a shallow dish. Layer the remaining pesto, 1/2 of the remaining cream cheese mixture, remaining bell pepper strips and remaining cream cheese mixture in a shallow dish. Spread the reserved pesto over the top. Garnish with the reserved bell pepper strips.

Serve with sliced Italian bread.

Menu

ROASTED PEPPER
PESTO DIP

⬚

TANGY FRUIT COLESLAW

⬚

PICNIC POTATO SALAD

⬚

BEAN AND EGGPLANT
SALAD

⬚

BROCCOLI PASTA SALAD

⬚

COMPANY FRIED
CHICKEN

⬚

CREAM BISCUITS

⬚

WHITE TEXAS SHEET
CAKE

⬚

LEMON BLUEBERRY PIE

⬚

CHOCOLATE ESPRESSO
COOKIES

Tangy Fruit Coleslaw

SERVES 20

3 pounds shredded cabbage
1 (10-ounce) can mandarin oranges,
    drained
1 McIntosh apple, cut into bite-size pieces
1 green bell pepper, chopped

1/2 to 1 cup mayonnaise
1/3 cup sugar
2 tablespoons white wine vinegar
2 tablespoons milk

DIRECTIONS:

Combine the cabbage, mandarin oranges, apple and bell pepper in a large
bowl and toss to mix well.

Mix the mayonnaise, sugar, vinegar and milk in a bowl until smooth. Pour
over the cabbage mixture and toss well.

Chill, covered, until ready to serve.

Picnic Potato Salad

SERVES 10 TO 12

8 large potatoes, peeled
10 hard-cooked eggs
1 tablespoon vinegar
1 tablespoon sugar
1 tablespoon prepared mustard
1 cup mayonnaise

1 cup sour cream
salt and pepper to taste
1 cucumber
3 ribs celery, chopped
6 radishes, chopped
1 bunch green onions, chopped

DIRECTIONS:

Boil the potatoes in water to cover in a saucepan until tender; drain. Let
stand until cool; chop the potatoes.

Separate the egg yolks from the egg whites. Combine the egg yolks,
vinegar, sugar and prepared mustard in a mixing bowl and blend well. Add
the mayonnaise and sour cream and mix well. Season with salt and pepper.

Cut the cucumber into halves lengthwise and remove the seeds. Cut into
slices. Chop the egg whites. Combine the potatoes, egg whites, cucumber,
celery, radishes and green onions in a large bowl and toss to mix well. Add
the egg yolk mixture and mix well. Chill, covered, until ready to serve.

Bean and Eggplant Salad

For a romantic touch, line your walkway or patio with votives.

3 cups canned Great Northern beans, drained

3 cups canned or cooked pinto beans, drained

3 cups canned red kidney beans, drained

1 cup minced green onions or chives

1/2 cup minced fresh parsley

2 garlic cloves, crushed

Mustard French Dressing (below)

2 cups (1-inch) cubed eggplant

flour for coating

salt and pepper to taste

1/4 cup olive oil

1 cup chopped seeded peeled tomatoes

DIRECTIONS:

Combine the beans, green onions, parsley and garlic in a large bowl and mix well. Stir in Mustard French Dressing. Chill, covered, for several hours.

Coat the eggplant lightly with flour, salt and pepper. Sauté in the olive oil in a skillet until light brown; drain. Let stand until cool.

Add the eggplant and tomatoes to the bean mixture and mix well. Chill, covered, for several hours before serving. Serve in an earthenware crock or bowl.

Note: You may substitute broiled lightly smoked sausage for the eggplant.

Mustard French Dressing

1/3 cup olive oil

1/3 cup vegetable oil

1/3 cup wine vinegar

1 tablespoon Dijon mustard

salt and pepper to taste

DIRECTIONS:

Whisk the olive oil, vegetable oil, vinegar, Dijon mustard, salt and pepper in a bowl until emulsified.

Broccoli Pasta Salad

To store broccoli, wrap it in a damp kitchen towel and refrigerate up to three days. Never store it in a plastic bag because humidity will build up, causing the broccoli to wilt faster.

16 ounces medium bow tie pasta or shell macaroni
1/2 cup olive oil
1/2 cup vegetable oil
1/2 cup vinegar
2 1/2 teaspoons salt
1 teaspoon Dijon mustard
1/2 teaspoon ground white pepper
1 cup grated Parmesan cheese
1 (2-ounce) jar diced pimento, drained
1 bunch fresh broccoli, cut into florets
salt to taste
1/2 cup pine nuts or slivered almonds, toasted

DIRECTIONS:

Cook the pasta using the package directions. Rinse with cold water and drain.

Process the olive oil, vegetable oil, vinegar, 2 1/2 teaspoons salt, Dijon mustard, white pepper and cheese in a food processor for 30 seconds or until blended.

Combine the pasta and pimento in a large bowl. Add the dressing and toss gently. Cover and let stand at room temperature for 4 hours. (You may prepare ahead up to this point and chill, covered, for up to 24 hours.)

Blanch the broccoli in salted boiling water in a large saucepan; drain and cool.

Combine the broccoli and 1/4 cup of the pine nuts with the pasta mixture and toss to mix. Sprinkle with the remaining pine nuts. Let stand at room temperature for 30 minutes before serving.

Company Fried Chicken

SERVES 36

6 cups flour
2 tablespoons baking powder
2 tablespoons salt
2 tablespoons pepper

6 cups flour
12 chickens, cut up
3 cups milk
shortening for frying

DIRECTIONS:

Mix 6 cups flour, baking powder, salt and pepper in a large bowl.

Place 6 cups flour in a large brown paper bag. Drop several pieces of chicken at a time into the sack and shake well to coat. Dip 1 piece of chicken at a time in the milk and roll in the seasoned flour mixture.

Preheat the oven to 250 degrees.

Brown the chicken on both sides in batches in the shortening in a large skillet. Arrange in baking pans lined with nonrecycled brown paper bags.

Bake for 25 to 30 minutes or until the chicken is tender and crisp.

Serve hot or cold.

Cream Biscuits

MAKES 1 DOZEN

2 cups flour
2 1/2 teaspoons baking powder
1/2 to 3/4 teaspoon salt

1 1/4 cups heavy cream
melted butter

DIRECTIONS:

Preheat the oven to 450 degrees.

Whisk the flour, baking powder and salt in a large bowl. Add the cream all at once. Mix just until most of the flour mixture is moistened. Shape the dough into a ball in the bowl with lightly floured hands. Knead gently against the side of the bowl for 5 to 10 minutes or until the bowl is fairly clean, turning and pressing any loose pieces into the dough.

Roll the dough 1/2 inch thick on a lightly floured surface. Cut into 2-inch squares or circles with a knife or biscuit cutter. Arrange 1 inch apart on a baking sheet. Brush with melted butter.

Bake on the middle oven rack for 10 to 12 minutes or until the biscuits are golden brown.

White Texas Sheet Cake

SERVES 24

1 cup (2 sticks) butter	2 eggs, beaten
1 cup water	1 teaspoon salt
2 cups flour	1 teaspoon baking powder
2 cups sugar	1 teaspoon almond extract
1/2 cup sour cream	Butter Pecan Frosting (below)

DIRECTIONS:

Preheat the oven to 350 degrees.

Bring the butter and water to a boil in a saucepan, stirring occasionally. Remove from the heat.

Add the flour, sugar, sour cream, eggs, salt, baking powder and almond extract and whisk until smooth. Spoon into a buttered and lightly floured 10×15-inch cake pan.

Bake for 20 to 25 minutes or until light brown. Remove from the oven. Spread the warm cake with Butter Pecan Frosting.

Butter Pecan Frosting

1/2 cup (1 stick) butter	3 cups confectioners' sugar
1/4 cup milk	1 cup chopped pecans
1/2 teaspoon almond extract	

DIRECTIONS:

Bring the butter and milk to a boil in a saucepan over medium heat, stirring occasionally. Remove from the heat. Whisk in the almond extract. Whisk in the confectioners' sugar gradually until of a spreading consistency. Stir in the pecans.

Lemon Blueberry Pie

1 (14-ounce) can sweetened condensed
   milk
juice of 2 lemons
1/2 cup whipping cream
1 cup pecans

1 1/2 cups fresh or frozen blueberries
1 baked (9-inch) pie shell
1/2 cup whipping cream
sugar to taste

DIRECTIONS:

Combine the condensed milk, lemon juice and 1/2 cup whipping cream in a
bowl and mix well. Stir in the pecans and blueberries. Pour into the pie shell.

Whip 1/2 cup whipping cream and sugar in a mixing bowl until soft peaks
form. Spread over the top of the pie, sealing to the edge.

Chill, covered, in the refrigerator until ready to serve.

Chocolate Espresso Cookies

6 tablespoons flour
1/4 teaspoon baking powder
1/4 teaspoon salt
8 ounces bittersweet or semisweet
   chocolate, chopped (1 rounded cup)
1/2 cup (1 stick) unsalted butter

2 eggs
3/4 cup sugar
2 1/2 teaspoons instant espresso powder
2 1/4 teaspoons vanilla extract
1 cup (6 ounces) semisweet chocolate chips
1 cup coarsely chopped walnuts

DIRECTIONS:

Preheat the oven to 350 degrees.

Mix the flour, baking powder and salt in a small bowl. Melt the
bittersweet chocolate and butter in a heavy saucepan over low heat, stirring
constantly. Remove from the heat.

Beat the eggs, sugar, espresso powder and vanilla in a medium mixing
bowl until blended. Stir into the warm chocolate mixture. Add the flour
mixture and mix well. Stir in the chocolate chips and walnuts. Drop by
heaping tablespoonfuls 1 1/2 inches apart onto nonstick cookie sheets.

Bake for 12 minutes or until the tops crack but the cookies are still moist
inside. Cool on the cookie sheets for 5 minutes. Remove to wire racks to cool
completely. Store in an airtight container at room temperature.

Note: You may prepare 1 day ahead.

ENGAGEMENT COCKTAIL PARTY

Toast the bride and groom at this elegant cocktail party. The menu consists of easy-to-eat but chic cuisine that is certain to appeal to everyone on the guest list.

Champagne Punch

SERVES 50

2 cups sugar
2 cups water
1/4 cup lemon juice
1 (6-ounce) can frozen orange juice
*   concentrate, thawed*
1 1/2 cups apple juice

2 cups pineapple juice
2 fifths Champagne
3 cups ginger ale

Garnish:
strawberries

DIRECTIONS:

Bring the sugar and water to a boil in a saucepan. Boil for 1 minute. Remove from the heat to cool.

Combine the lemon juice, orange juice concentrate, apple juice and pineapple juice in a punch bowl and mix well. Stir in the sugar mixture. (You may prepare ahead up to this point and freeze until ready to serve.)

Add the Champagne and ginger ale just before serving and mix well. Add ice and garnish with strawberries. Ladle into 4-ounce punch cups.

Greek Olive Cups

MAKES 30

1 cup chopped pecans, toasted
1 cup (4 ounces) shredded Cheddar cheese
1 cup chopped pimento-stuffed olives

2 tablespoons mayonnaise
2 (15-count) packages frozen miniature
*   phyllo shells*

DIRECTIONS:

Mix the pecans, cheese, olives and mayonnaise in a bowl. Spoon 1 teaspoon of the mixture into each shell. (You may store in the freezer until ready to serve.)

Preheat the oven to 375 degrees.

Arrange on a baking sheet. (If frozen, let stand for 10 minutes.)

Bake for 12 to 15 minutes or until golden brown.

Toasted Walnuts

MAKES 2 CUPS

2 cups walnut halves
1/4 teaspoon salt

1/8 teaspoon cayenne pepper
2 teaspoons walnut oil

DIRECTIONS:

Preheat the oven to 300 degrees.

Drop the walnuts into rapidly boiling water in a saucepan. Boil for 1 minute; drain. Place on a clean towel. Rub gently to remove the paper thin skins. Spread on a baking sheet. Sprinkle with the salt, cayenne pepper and walnut oil.

Bake for 13 to 15 minutes or until golden brown, stirring occasionally. Watch carefully to prevent burning. Remove from the oven and cool to room temperature. Store in an airtight container in the refrigerator.

Quick and Simple Pesto Pie

SERVES 12

2 (1-crust) pie pastries
1 cup (4 ounces) shredded Pepper Jack
   cheese
1/2 cup prepared pesto

milk
pine nuts
paprika

DIRECTIONS:

Preheat the oven to 400 degrees.

Bring the pie pastries to room temperature. Arrange 1 pie pastry in the center of a lightly floured baking sheet.

Bake for 8 to 10 minutes or until the pastry begins to brown.

Combine the cheese and pesto in a bowl and mix well. Spread evenly over the hot pastry to within 1/2 inch of the edge. Top with the remaining pastry, sealing the edges with a fork and cutting vents in the top to allow the steam to escape. Brush with milk. Sprinkle liberally with pine nuts and press into the pastry. Sprinkle liberally with paprika.

Bake for 15 to 18 minutes or until golden brown. Remove from the oven. Let stand for 10 minutes.

Arrange on a serving platter. Cut into 12 wedges; cut each wedge into halves by cutting a circle halfway between the edge and center. Serve warm.

ONION, CHEESE AND
BASIL TART

PROSCIUTTO-WRAPPED
ASPARAGUS

HEARTS OF PALM
SPREAD

EASY OLIVE BREAD

MARBLED FUDGE BARS

KEY LIME BARS

PECAN DAINTIES

Lamb Riblets

SERVES 10

4 to 5 pounds lamb riblets
1 1/2 teaspoons seasoned salt
1 1/2 teaspoons garlic salt

1 1/2 teaspoons salt
1 1/2 teaspoons pepper
2 tablespoons Worcestershire sauce

DIRECTIONS:

Preheat the broiler.

Cut the riblets between each rib. Arrange on a rack in a broiler pan.

Mix the seasoned salt, garlic salt, salt, pepper and Worcestershire sauce in a small bowl. Brush over the lamb.

Broil 6 inches from the heat source until brown, turning frequently. (You may prepare ahead up to this point.)

Preheat the oven to 375 degrees.

Bake for 30 minutes or until cooked through.

Bombay Chicken Bites

SERVES 24

1 whole chicken breast, skinned and
    boned
3 green onions
salt to taste
3 ounces cream cheese, softened

1 teaspoon curry powder, or to taste
1 tablespoon mayonnaise
2 tablespoons chutney, chopped
1 cup dry roasted peanuts, chopped
sliced preserved ginger

DIRECTIONS:

Poach the chicken with the green onions and salt in water to cover in a saucepan for 25 minutes; drain. Cut the chicken into 1-inch pieces.

Process the chicken, cream cheese, curry powder and mayonnaise in a food processor until smooth. Stir in the chutney.

Shape into bite-size balls. Roll in the chopped peanuts. Arrange on a tray. Top each with a slice of ginger.

Note: You may prepare a day ahead and store in the refrigerator or freezer.

Shrimp Tarts

MAKES 3 DOZEN

When preparing fish dishes, the key is to use fresh fish—never frozen.

6 cups water
2 pounds large fresh shrimp
2/3 cup finely chopped green onions
1/2 cup finely chopped fresh parsley
2/3 cup mayonnaise
2 tablespoons capers
1 teaspoon salt

1/4 teaspoon red pepper
1 garlic clove, minced
Tart Shells (below)

Garnish:
diagonally sliced green onions

DIRECTIONS:

Bring the water to a boil in a saucepan. Add the shrimp. Cook for 3 to 5 minutes or until the shrimp turn pink. Drain well and rinse with cold water. Chill, covered, in the refrigerator. Peel, devein and coarsely chop the shrimp.

Combine the shrimp, 2/3 cup green onions, parsley, mayonnaise, capers, salt, red pepper and garlic in a large bowl and mix well. Spoon into Tart Shells. Garnish with diagonally sliced green onions.

Tart Shells

1/2 cup (1 stick) butter, softened
4 ounces cream cheese, softened
1 1/4 cups flour

1/4 cup grated asiago cheese
1/4 teaspoon salt

DIRECTIONS:

Combine the butter and cream cheese in a bowl and mix until blended. Add the flour, asiago cheese and salt and blend well. Divide the dough into 3 equal portions. Chill, covered, in the refrigerator.

Preheat the oven to 350 degrees.

Shape each portion of dough into 12 balls. Press each ball into lightly greased 1 3/4-inch miniature muffin cups.

Bake for 15 to 17 minutes or until golden brown. Cool and remove from the cups.

Onion, Cheese and Basil Tart

2 medium red onions, unpeeled and cut
  into 12 wedges
3 tablespoons olive oil
salt and pepper to taste
1 sheet frozen puff pastry, thawed
1 egg, beaten

8 ounces soft fresh goat cheese, such as
  Montrachet
1/4 cup prepared pesto
1/4 cup whipping cream
3 tablespoons chopped fresh basil

DIRECTIONS:

Preheat the oven to 400 degrees.

Toss the unpeeled onion wedges with olive oil in a medium bowl. Season with salt and pepper. Arrange in a single layer on an oiled large heavy baking sheet.

Bake for 25 minutes or until tender and the bottoms are golden brown. Cool on a wire rack. (You may prepare 1 day ahead. Cover and let stand at room temperature.)

Preheat the oven to 400 degrees.

Roll the pastry into an 11×14-inch rectangle on a lightly floured surface. Trim the edges to even. Cut a 1/2-inch strip from each side of the pastry to form a 10×13-inch rectangle, reserving the strips. Arrange the rectangle on a large heavy baking sheet. Brush the edges with some of the beaten egg. Place the strips on the edges to create a border, trimming and pressing gently to adhere. Pierce the bottom of the pastry several times with a fork.

Bake for 15 minutes or until the edges puff and the pastry is golden brown. Remove the baking sheet to a wire rack. Loosen the pastry from the baking sheet with a metal spatula. Cool on the baking sheet.

Reduce the oven temperature to 350 degrees.

Combine the goat cheese, pesto, whipping cream and 2 tablespoons of the basil in a medium bowl and stir until smooth. Season with salt and pepper. Stir in the remaining beaten egg. Spread evenly over the bottom of the crust.

Remove the peel and stem end from the roasted onions. Fan the wedges, golden brown side up, over the cheese mixture.

Bake for 20 minutes or until the cheese appears set and the crust is brown. Cool on the baking sheet on a wire rack. Sprinkle with the remaining basil. Cut into squares.

Prosciutto-Wrapped Asparagus

SERVES 4

12 to 16 asparagus spears, depending on
    the size
1/2 teaspoon salt
3 ounces provolone cheese, cut into
    quarters lengthwise

2 thin slices prosciutto, cut into halves
    lengthwise
8 (1/8×2-inch) slices roasted red
    bell pepper

DIRECTIONS:

Trim the woody bases from the asparagus. Blanch the asparagus in rapidly boiling salted water in a saucepan for 1 minute or until tender-crisp; drain. Plunge immediately into cold water to stop the cooking process; drain.

Place 1 piece of cheese in the middle of 3 or 4 asparagus pieces. Wrap the proscuitto around the middle. Repeat to form 3 more bundles. Arrange in a microwavable dish and cover with plastic wrap. (You may prepare ahead and chill for up to 4 hours.)

Microwave on High for 3 minutes or until the cheese melts. Remove the plastic wrap. Arrange the bell pepper crisscrossed on top of the prosciutto. Serve immediately.

Store fresh asparagus in the refrigerator with the cut ends upright in about an inch of cold water.

Hearts of Palm Spread

MAKES 2 CUPS

1 (14-ounce) can hearts of palm, drained
    and chopped
1 cup (4 ounces) shredded mozzarella
    cheese

3/4 cup mayonnaise
1/2 cup grated Parmesan cheese
1/4 cup sour cream
1 green onion, minced

DIRECTIONS:

Preheat the oven to 350 degrees.

Combine the hearts of palm, mozzarella cheese, mayonnaise, Parmesan cheese, sour cream and green onion in a bowl and mix well. Spoon into a lightly greased 9-inch quiche dish or pie plate.

Bake, uncovered, for 20 minutes or until hot and bubbly. Serve with melba rounds.

Easy Olive Bread

SERVES 16

2 loaves frozen bread dough
1 (5-ounce) jar pimento-stuffed olives

olive oil cooking spray
2 tablespoons coarse sea salt

DIRECTIONS:

Thaw the bread dough in the refrigerator for 8 to 12 hours.

Drain the olives and place on a paper towel to absorb the moisture.

Preheat the oven to 375 degrees.

Place 1 loaf of the dough on a baking sheet sprayed with olive oil cooking spray. Flatten into an oval shape about 1/2 inch thick with oiled hands. Press 1/2 of the olives into the dough, distributing evenly over the top. Spray with olive oil cooking spray. Sprinkle with the sea salt. Repeat with the remaining dough and olives.

Bake for 30 to 35 minutes or until light brown. Remove from the oven. Cool for a few minutes before cutting into pieces.

Marbled Fudge Bars

MAKES 3 DOZEN

1 cup (2 sticks) butter or margarine
4 ounces semisweet chocolate
2 cups sugar
3 eggs
1 cup flour
1/2 teaspoon salt

1 cup chopped walnuts
2 teaspoons vanilla extract
8 ounces cream cheese, softened
1/2 cup sugar
1 egg
2 teaspoons vanilla extract

DIRECTIONS:

Preheat the oven to 350 degrees.

Melt the butter and chocolate in a 2-quart heavy saucepan over low heat. Remove from the heat. Add 2 cups sugar and 3 eggs and beat until well blended. Stir in the flour, salt, walnuts and 2 teaspoons vanilla. Spread evenly in a greased and floured 9×13-inch baking pan.

Combine the cream cheese, 1/2 cup sugar, 1 egg and 2 teaspoons vanilla in a mixing bowl and beat at low speed until blended. Beat at medium speed for 2 minutes. Dollop on top of the chocolate batter. Score the surface in a criss-cross pattern using the tip of a knife.

Bake for 40 to 45 minutes or until a wooden pick inserted in the center comes out clean.

Note: You may store in the refrigerator for up to 1 week.

Key Lime Bars

MAKES 1¹⁄₃ DOZEN

With larger, formal gatherings, label your dishes for your guests to add a nice touch.

¹⁄₂ cup (1 stick) butter or margarine,
   softened
1 cup sifted flour
¹⁄₄ cup confectioners' sugar

³⁄₄ cup sugar
2 tablespoons flour
2 eggs
¹⁄₄ cup Key lime juice

DIRECTIONS:

Preheat the oven to 350 degrees.

Combine the butter, 1 cup flour and the confectioners' sugar in a mixing bowl and beat well. Press the dough into the bottom of an ungreased 8×8-inch baking pan.

Bake for 20 minutes or until light brown.

Beat the sugar, 2 tablespoons flour, eggs and lime juice in a mixing bowl until smooth. Pour over the baked layer.

Bake for 20 minutes or until set. Cool in the pan on a wire rack. Cut into bars.

Note: For added sweetness, sprinkle with about 1 teaspoon confectioners' sugar. These bars taste even better the second day and also freeze well.

Pecan Dainties

MAKES 4 DOZEN

6 ounces cream cheese, softened
1 cup (2 sticks) margarine, softened
2 cups flour
1¹⁄₂ cups (about) finely chopped pecans
3 eggs, lightly beaten

2 cups packed brown sugar
2 tablespoons margarine, melted
1 teaspoon vanilla extract
dash of salt

DIRECTIONS:

Preheat the oven to 350 degrees.

Combine the cream cheese, 1 cup margarine and flour in a bowl and mix well. Shape into small balls. Press into miniature muffin cups. Sprinkle a few pecans in each cup.

Combine the eggs, brown sugar, 2 tablespoons margarine, vanilla and salt in a bowl and mix well. Fill each lined muffin cup ¹⁄₂ full. Sprinkle with pecans.

Bake for 20 minutes. Cool on wire racks.

FAMILY REUNION

Share special moments and family stories as you gather at the Family Reunion. Dish out warmth and love while serving a delicious home-style meal.

Almond Tea

SERVES 8 TO 10

1 cup strong brewed tea
1 cup lemon juice
2 cups sugar or equivalent of sugar
  substitute

2 tablespoons almond extract
1 tablespoon vanilla extract
4 cups water
1 (2-liter) bottle ginger ale, chilled

DIRECTIONS:

Combine the tea, lemon juice, sugar, almond flavoring, vanilla and water in a large pitcher and mix well. Chill, covered, until ready to serve.

To serve, stir in the chilled ginger ale. Serve over ice in tall glasses.

Curry Cheese Ball

SERVES 10 TO 12

11 ounces cream cheese, softened
2 tablespoons sour cream
1 tablespoon curry powder
1/2 cup salted peanut halves
1/2 cup bacon bits

1/2 cup chopped green onions
1/2 cup raisins or golden raisins
1 (11-ounce) jar chutney, such as Major
  Grey's mango chutney

DIRECTIONS:

Beat the cream cheese, sour cream and curry powder in a mixing bowl until smooth and creamy. Add the peanuts, bacon bits, green onions and raisins and mix well. Shape into a ball.

Chill, covered, until firm.

To serve, drizzle the chutney over the top and side of the cheese ball. Serve with thick crackers.

PHOTOGRAPH LEFT: TOMATO, BASIL AND MOZZARELLA SKEWERS

Cabbage Salad for a Crowd

SERVES 25 TO 30

3¹/2 pounds cabbage, shredded
3 cups sliced celery
3 cups chopped onions
1 green bell pepper, chopped
1 red bell pepper, chopped
2 cups white vinegar
1 cup water

2 cups sugar
2 tablespoons garlic powder
2 tablespoons mustard seeds
1 tablespoon celery seeds
1 tablespoon turmeric
1 tablespoon salt

DIRECTIONS:

Combine the cabbage, celery, onions and bell peppers in a large bowl or crock and mix well.

Bring the vinegar, water, sugar, garlic powder, mustard seeds, celery seeds, turmeric and salt to a boil in a saucepan. Pour over the vegetable mixture and stir 2 or 3 times. Chill in the refrigerator for 24 hours before serving. Store in the refrigerator for up to 1 month.

Couscous Salad with Cinnamon Vinaigrette

SERVES 6 TO 8

1/3 cup canola oil
2 teaspoons cinnamon
1 teaspoon cumin
2¹/3 cups vegetable or chicken broth
1 (10-ounce) package couscous
3/4 cup dried cranberries
3 tablespoons minced shallots

2 tablespoons white wine vinegar
5 green onions, chopped
1 (15-ounce) can chick-peas, rinsed
    and drained
5 tablespoons fresh cilantro or mint,
    chopped
salt and pepper to taste

DIRECTIONS:

Bring the canola oil, cinnamon and cumin to a boil in a saucepan, stirring constantly. Remove from the heat to cool.

Bring the broth to a boil in a saucepan. Stir in the couscous and dried cranberries. Cover and remove from the heat. Let stand for 5 minutes. Fluff with a fork. Let stand until cool.

Whisk the shallots and vinegar into the cinnamon mixture. Pour over the couscous mixture. Add the green onions, chick-peas and cilantro and mix well. Season with salt and pepper. Serve at room temperature or chilled.

Sweet-and-Sour Fruit Salad

—❧—

Serves 12 to 15

For a special touch, roll your guests' napkins, tie with ribbon, and add sprigs of fresh flowers or herbs.

1 pineapple

4 bananas, sliced

4 large red apples, unpeeled and coarsely chopped

3 oranges, peeled, seeded and sectioned

2 cups seedless green grapes

Sweet-and-Sour Fruit Dressing (below)

DIRECTIONS:

Cut the pineapple into quarters lengthwise. Cut the pineapple away from the skin and into bite-size pieces, discarding the core.

Combine the pineapple, bananas, apples, oranges and grapes in a large bowl. Add Sweet-and-Sour Fruit Dressing and toss gently to coat. Chill, covered, until ready to serve.

Sweet-and-Sour Fruit Dressing

4 egg yolks

1 1/2 cups sugar

1/2 cup milk

1 teaspoon dry mustard

1/2 cup vinegar

DIRECTIONS:

Combine the egg yolks, sugar, milk and dry mustard in a medium saucepan and mix well.

Cook over low heat until smooth and thickened, stirring constantly. Stir in the vinegar.

Remove from the heat to cool.

Corn Casserole

1 (11-ounce) can whole kernel corn
1 (17-ounce) can cream-style corn
1/4 cup sugar
3/4 cup corn bread mix

1 egg, beaten
1 cup sour cream
chopped jalapeño chiles to taste
2 cups (8 ounces) shredded Cheddar cheese

DIRECTIONS:

Preheat the oven to 350 degrees.

Combine the whole kernel corn, cream-style corn, sugar, corn bread mix, egg, sour cream and jalapeño chiles in a large bowl and mix well. Spoon into a nonstick 9×13-inch baking pan.

Bake for 45 minutes. Sprinkle with the cheese. Bake until melted.

Beef Brisket

SERVES 10 TO 12

1 (5- to 7-pound) beef brisket
1 1/2 (10-ounce) bottles soy sauce
1 (10-ounce) can beef consommé
1 tablespoon vinegar

1 tablespoon liquid smoke
1 garlic clove, finely chopped
1/2 cup water

DIRECTIONS:

Place the beef in a large sealable plastic bag. Combine the soy sauce, consommé, vinegar, liquid smoke and garlic in a bowl and mix well. Pour over the beef and seal the bag.

Marinate in the refrigerator for 24 hours.

Preheat the oven to 300 degrees.

Drain the beef, reserving 1 cup of the marinade. Arrange the beef in a large covered baking dish. Add the reserved marinade and water.

Bake, covered, for 4 to 5 hours or until tender, basting occasionally with the pan juices. Cool before cutting into thin slices.

Buffalo Chip Cookies

MAKES 3 DOZEN

4 cups flour
1 teaspoon salt
2 teaspoons baking soda
2 teaspoons baking powder
2 cups quick-cooking oats
2 cups crushed cornflakes
2 cups (12 ounces) chocolate chips
1 cup chopped pecans

1 cup shredded coconut
2 cups (4 sticks) butter or margarine,
   softened
2 cups packed brown sugar
2 cups sugar
4 eggs, lightly beaten
2 teaspoons vanilla extract

DIRECTIONS:

Preheat the oven to 350 degrees.

Mix the flour, salt, baking soda and baking powder together. Mix the oats, cornflakes, chocolate chips, pecans and coconut in a bowl.

Cream the butter, brown sugar and sugar in a large mixing bowl until light and fluffy. Beat in the eggs and vanilla. Add the flour mixture and mix well. Stir in the oat mixture. Drop the dough by ice cream scoopfuls onto lightly greased cookie sheets, allowing 6 cookies per sheet.

Bake for 7 to 10 minutes.

Note: The cookies will be soft and chewy if not baked until brown.

To ensure even baking, leave at least two inches of space between baking pans and the sides of the oven and door. This will allow air to circulate.

Fresh Peach Pie

2¹/2 to 3 cups sliced peeled fresh peaches
juice of 1/2 lemon
1 cup sour cream
1 teaspoon vanilla extract
2¹/2 (heaping) tablespoons flour
1 egg, lightly beaten
3/4 to 1 cup sugar

pinch of salt
1 unbaked (10-inch) pie shell
3 tablespoons butter, cut into pieces
2 tablespoons flour
3 tablespoons chopped walnuts or pecans
3 tablespoons brown sugar

DIRECTIONS:

Preheat the oven to 400 degrees.

Combine the peaches, lemon juice, sour cream, vanilla, 2¹/2 heaping tablespoons flour, egg, sugar and salt in a large bowl and mix well. Pour into the pie shell.

Bake for 25 minutes.

Mix the butter, 2 tablespoons flour, walnuts and brown sugar in a bowl until crumbly. Sprinkle over the pie.

Bake for 5 to 10 minutes or until brown.

Blueberry Crunch

SERVES 10

4 cups fresh blueberries
1 cup packed brown sugar
1/4 cup flour

3/4 cup rolled oats
1/4 cup (1/2 stick) margarine, melted

DIRECTIONS:

Preheat the oven to 350 degrees.

Spread the blueberries evenly in a 2-quart baking dish.

Combine the brown sugar, flour, oats and margarine in a bowl and mix well. Sprinkle over the blueberries.

Bake for 45 minutes.

Serve warm with vanilla ice cream or frozen yogurt.

BIRTHDAY BRUNCH

Celebrate someone you love with this delicious brunch menu. You will help your Guest of Honor start the next year in a warm and fun way.

Honey Brunch Mimosas

SERVES 6

1 (6-ounce) can frozen lemonade
concentrate, thawed
1/4 cup Grand Marnier or other
orange-flavored liqueur
1/4 cup honey, warmed

1 (750-milliliter) bottle dry Champagne,
chilled

Garnish:
fresh strawberries

DIRECTIONS:

Combine the lemonade concentrate and Grand Marnier in a large pitcher and mix well. Add the warmed honey and stir until dissolved. Stir in the Champagne just before serving.

Pour into individual Champagne glasses. Garnish with strawberries.

Mixed Greens with Grapefruit Vinaigrette

SERVES 4

1 small grapefruit, or 1 large navel
orange, peeled and sectioned
1 small shallot
2 teaspoons extra-virgin olive oil
2 teaspoons raspberry vinegar or
white wine vinegar

1 tablespoon chopped fresh chives
freshly ground pepper to taste
assorted mixed greens

DIRECTIONS:

Process the grapefruit, shallot, olive oil and vinegar in a blender or food processor until smooth. Stir in the chives. Season with pepper. (The vinaigrette may be prepared up to 3 days ahead and stored, covered, in the refrigerator.)

Place the mixed salad greens in a salad bowl. Add the desired amount of vinaigrette and toss to coat.

Cheesy Apple Bacon Strata

3 tablespoons butter or margarine

3 medium Granny Smith apples, peeled
    and coarsely chopped (3 cups)

3 tablespoons brown sugar

4 cups cubed firm bread (7 slices)

1 pound bacon, crisp-cooked and crumbled

2 cups (8 ounces) shredded sharp Cheddar
    cheese

2½ cups milk

5 eggs

1 tablespoon dry mustard

2 teaspoons Worcestershire sauce

¼ teaspoon salt

⅛ teaspoon pepper

DIRECTIONS:

Melt the butter in a 10-inch skillet over medium heat. Add the apples. Cook
for 2 to 3 minutes or until tender-crisp, stirring occasionally. Stir in the
brown sugar. Reduce the heat to low. Cook for 5 to 6 minutes or until the
apples are tender, stirring occasionally.

Layer the bread, bacon, apple mixture and cheese ½ at a time in a greased
2-quart baking dish. Combine the milk, eggs, dry mustard, Worcestershire
sauce, salt and pepper in a bowl and mix well. Pour over the layers.

Chill, tightly covered, for 2 to 24 hours.

Preheat the oven to 350 degrees.

Bake, uncovered, for 40 to 45 minutes or until a knife inserted in the
center comes out clean. Let stand for 10 minutes before serving.

Brie and Sausage Breakfast Casserole

When cooking in a glass dish, reduce the oven temperature by twenty-five degrees. Food in glass dishes cooks faster than in metal pans.

SERVES 10 TO 12

1 (8-ounce) wheel Brie cheese

1 pound hot bulk pork sausage

6 slices white bread

1 cup grated Parmesan cheese

5 eggs

2 cups whipping cream

2 cups fat-free milk

1 tablespoon sage

1 teaspoon salt

1 teaspoon pepper

2 eggs

1 cup whipping cream

DIRECTIONS:

Trim the rind from the Brie cheese and discard. Cut the Brie cheese into cubes.

Brown the sausage in a large skillet over medium heat, stirring until crumbly; drain.

Trim the crusts from the bread. Arrange the bread in a lightly greased 9×13-inch baking dish. Layer the sausage, Brie cheese and Parmesan cheese evenly over the bread.

Whisk 5 eggs, 2 cups whipping cream, milk, sage, salt and pepper in a bowl. Pour evenly over the layers. Chill, covered, for 8 hours.

Preheat the oven to 350 degrees.

Whisk 2 eggs and 1 cup whipping cream in a bowl. Pour over the chilled mixture.

Bake for 1 hour or until set.

Cheese Danish

SERVES 16

2 (8-count) cans crescent rolls
16 ounces cream cheese, softened
3/4 cup sugar
1 egg yolk

1 teaspoon vanilla extract
1 egg white, lightly beaten
1 cup confectioners' sugar
milk

DIRECTIONS:

Preheat the oven to 350 degrees.

Unroll 1 can of the crescent roll dough. Fit in the bottom of a greased 9×13-inch baking pan, pressing the perforations to seal.

Beat the cream cheese, sugar, egg yolk and vanilla in a mixing bowl until smooth. Spread over the dough. Unroll the remaining crescent roll dough, pressing the perforations to seal. Arrange over the cream cheese layer. Brush with the beaten egg white.

Bake for 30 minutes.

Beat the confectioners' sugar with enough milk in a bowl to make of a glaze consistency. Spread over the top.

Strawberry Bread

MAKES 2 LOAVES

2 (10-ounce) packages frozen
    strawberries, thawed
4 eggs or an equivalent amount of egg
    substitute
1¼ cups vegetable oil
3 cups flour

1 teaspoon baking soda
1/2 teaspoon salt
1 tablespoon cinnamon
2 cups sugar
1¼ cups chopped pecans (optional)

DIRECTIONS:

Preheat the oven to 350 degrees.

Mix the undrained strawberries, eggs and oil in a large bowl. Add the flour, baking soda, salt, cinnamon and sugar and mix well. Stir in the pecans. Pour into 2 greased 5×9-inch loaf pans.

Bake for 1 hour and 10 minutes or until a wooden pick inserted in the centers comes out clean. Cool in the pans for 10 minutes. Invert onto wire racks to cool completely.

Note: You may also bake in 3 medium loaf pans or 4 small loaf pans.

Nutty Orange Coffee Cake

SERVES 16

3/4 cup sugar
1/2 cup chopped pecans
2 tablespoons grated orange zest
2 (10-count) cans refrigerated
   buttermilk biscuits

8 ounces cream cheese, softened
1/2 cup (1 stick) butter, melted
1 cup sifted confectioners' sugar
2 tablespoons fresh orange juice

DIRECTIONS:

Preheat the oven to 350 degrees.

Mix the sugar, pecans and orange zest in a shallow dish.

Split the biscuits horizontally into halves. Spread each half with about 1 teaspoon of the cream cheese. Fold in half and press the edge to seal. Dip each in the butter. Roll in the sugar mixture. Arrange curved side down in a bundt pan. Drizzle the remaining butter over the top. Sprinkle with the remaining sugar mixture.

Bake for 45 to 55 minutes or until brown. Invert immediately onto a serving plate. Drizzle with a mixture of the confectioners' sugar and orange juice. Serve hot.

Running late with no time to iron napkins or do a complicated napkin fold? Pick the napkin up from its center and place the center in a glass. It looks great and adds dimension to your table setting.

Summer's Best Genuine English Trifle

Have fun with your centerpieces, but never allow them to overwhelm your table. Centerpieces should never block the view of guests.

1 package prepared shortcake shells or
    sponge cake
fruit of choice, such as bananas,
    strawberries, kiwifruit, blackberries,
    blueberries or raspberries
lemon juice

raspberry jam
cream sherry or brandy
Custard Filling (below)
sweetened whipped cream
Garnish:
fresh strawberries

DIRECTIONS:

Cut the round shortcake shells into halves or the sponge cake into pieces. Toss the fruit with lemon juice in a bowl to prevent the fruit from turning brown.

Line the bottom of a clear glass trifle bowl with 1/3 to 1/2 of the cake pieces. Spread with raspberry jam. Drizzle with the sherry. Add a layer of the fruit and a layer of the Custard Filling. Repeat the layers until the bowl is full. Spread the whipped cream over the top. Garnish with fresh strawberries.

Custard Filling

3/4 cup sugar
3 tablespoons cornstarch
1/8 teaspoon salt
1 cup milk
1 cup heavy cream

4 egg yolks, beaten
2 tablespoons butter
1 1/2 teaspoons vanilla extract
1 cup whipped cream

DIRECTIONS:

Mix the sugar, cornstarch and salt in the top of a double boiler. Add the milk and heavy cream gradually, stirring constantly.

Cook over hot water for 20 minutes or until thickened, stirring constantly.

Pour a small amount of the hot mixture into the beaten egg yolks in a bowl. Stir the egg yolks into the hot mixture. Add the butter and vanilla. Cook for 2 minutes, stirring frequently. (The mixture should be smooth. If lumps develop, strain through a sieve.) Fold in the whipped cream. Pour into a large bowl.

Chill, covered, in the refrigerator.

Fall

❧

IT SEEMS TO ME THAT OUR THREE BASIC NEEDS, FOR
FOOD AND SECURITY AND LOVE,
ARE SO ENTWINED THAT WE CANNOT THINK OF
ONE WITHOUT THE OTHER.
—M. F. K. Fisher

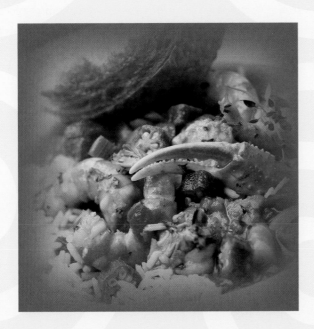

There is a special kind of excitement and energy in the fall. Fall conjures

up images of spectacular shows of turning leaves. There is a crispness in

the autumn air that speeds your step and takes your breath away.

Celebrate fall with the menus that follow. Anticipate the thrill of the

big game as you Tailgate with friends. Enjoy a warm Italian dinner

with the Texas Tuscan menu. Carve pumpkins at the Pumpkin Supper.

Or, treat your friends to a special evening with an Elegant Dinner Party.

There are so many ways to enjoy fall—just be sure that you do!

TAILGATE PARTY

With the crispness of fall, thoughts turn toward two great American traditions—football and tailgating. Enjoy the pregame festivities with these easy-to-transport or make-on-the-spot recipes.

Fiesta Dip

SERVES 18 TO 20

1 (10-ounce) package corn chips, crushed
1/4 cup (1/2 stick) butter or margarine, melted
2 (16-ounce) cans refried beans
1 envelope taco seasoning mix
1 (6-ounce) container frozen avocado dip, thawed
1 cup sour cream
3 (2-ounce) cans sliced black olives, drained
2 medium tomatoes, seeded and chopped
2 (4-ounce) cans chopped green chiles, drained
2 cups (8 ounces) shredded Pepper Jack cheese

Garnish:
sprigs of fresh cilantro

DIRECTIONS:

Preheat the oven to 350 degrees.

Combine the corn chips and butter in a bowl and toss to coat. Press on the bottom and 1 inch up the side of a lightly greased 9-inch springform pan.

Bake for 10 minutes. Cool on a wire rack.

Mix the refried beans and taco seasoning mix in a bowl. Spread over the baked layer. Continue layering with the avocado dip, sour cream, olives, tomatoes, green chiles and cheese. Chill, covered, for 8 hours.

To serve, place on a serving plate and remove the sides of the pan. Garnish with cilantro. Serve with large corn chips.

Teriyaki Drumettes

SERVES 12 TO 15

3 tablespoons soy sauce

3 tablespoons dry cooking sherry

30 chicken wing drumettes

3/4 cup teriyaki baste and glaze

1 garlic clove, minced

2 tablespoons sesame seeds, toasted

DIRECTIONS:

Preheat the oven to 425 degrees.

Blend the soy sauce and sherry in a large bowl. Add the chicken and turn until well coated. Arrange in a single layer in a large foil-lined baking pan.

Bake for 30 minutes.

Combine the glaze and garlic in a small bowl. Remove the chicken from the oven. Brush with 1/2 of the glaze mixture. Turn the chicken and baste with the remaining glaze mixture.

Bake for 15 minutes or until the chicken is cooked through. Sprinkle with the sesame seeds just before serving.

End of Summer Salad

SERVES 6

3 ears of white corn

6 ounces green beans, cut into 1-inch
    lengths

1/2 cup white wine vinegar

6 tablespoons vegetable oil

5 tablespoons sugar

3 tomatoes, seeded and chopped

1/2 cup chopped red onion

1/3 cup chopped fresh parsley

DIRECTIONS:

Shuck the corn, discarding the husks and silks. Cut the corn kernels from the cob into a bowl.

Cook the green beans in boiling water to cover in a saucepan for 2 minutes. Add the corn kernels. Cook for 2 minutes; drain well.

Whisk the vinegar, oil and sugar in a large bowl until blended. Add the green bean mixture, tomatoes, onion and parsley and toss to coat.

Chill, covered for 2 to 12 hours. Drain before serving if desired.

When serving a variety of salads, serve the dressings in old-fashioned cruets. Cruets can be found at antique shops and flea markets in pressed glass and cut crystal.

Tailgate Chili

2 pounds chuck steak, cut into bite-size
    pieces
1 pound hot Italian sausage, casings
    removed
2 large onions, chopped
12 garlic cloves, minced
1 tablespoon cumin
1 tablespoon paprika
1 tablespoon chili powder

2 (28-ounce) cans crushed tomatoes
1 (16-ounce) can pinto beans
1 (16-ounce) can Northern beans
1 (11-ounce) can dark red kidney beans

Garnishes:
chopped scallions
sour cream
shredded Cheddar cheese

DIRECTIONS:

Brown the beef and sausage in a large Dutch oven. Remove the beef mixture to a bowl using a slotted spoon. Drain the Dutch oven, reserving 2 tablespoons of the drippings.

Sauté the onions and garlic in the drippings for 7 to 8 minutes or until translucent. Add the cumin, paprika and chili powder. Stir in the tomatoes. Return the beef mixture to the Dutch oven and stir to mix well.

Bring to a boil and reduce the heat. Simmer for 1 1/2 hours. Add the beans. Simmer for 30 minutes.

Ladle into soup bowls. Garnish with scallions, sour cream and Cheddar cheese.

Corn and Crab Chowder

SERVES 4 TO 6

8 ounces bacon, chopped
2 onions, chopped
2 garlic cloves, minced
1/4 cup flour
4 1/2 cups milk
2 1/2 cups whole kernel corn
1 green bell pepper, chopped

1 teaspoon salt
1/2 teaspoon white pepper
1/2 teaspoon cayenne pepper
1 teaspoon thyme
1 pound crab meat, shells removed
    and flaked
juice of 1 lemon

Cold water brings out flavor and hot water seals it in. Therefore, always start a stock with cold water.

DIRECTIONS:

Fry the bacon in a 4-quart saucepan over medium heat until the bacon is crisp. Remove the bacon with a slotted spoon to paper towels to drain.

Sauté the onions in the bacon drippings for 3 to 4 minutes or until translucent. Add the garlic. Sauté for 2 minutes. Whisk in the flour. Cook for 2 minutes, whisking constantly. Whisk in the milk. Cook for 2 to 3 minutes or until slightly thickened, whisking constantly.

Stir in the corn, bell pepper, salt, white pepper, cayenne pepper and thyme. Bring to a boil and reduce the heat. Simmer for 6 to 8 minutes. Stir in the crab meat, bacon and lemon juice. Cook over low heat for 3 to 5 minutes or until heated through.

Fill-Me-Up with Garlic Cheese Loaf

SERVES 6 TO 8

To make garlic oil for cooking, peel and mash three garlic cloves. Place in a sterilized one-pint jar. Fill the jar with olive oil. Store the oil in a cool dark place. It will last for months.

1 (1-pound) loaf French bread
1/2 cup (1 stick) butter
6 garlic cloves, crushed
2 tablespoons sesame seeds
1 1/2 cups sour cream
2 cups cubed Monterey Jack cheese
1/2 cup grated Parmesan cheese
2 tablespoons parsley flakes

2 teaspoons lemon pepper
1 (14-ounce) can artichoke hearts,
    drained and coarsley chopped
1 cup (4 ounces) shredded Cheddar cheese

Garnishes:
tomato slices
sprigs of fresh parsley

DIRECTIONS:

Preheat the oven to 350 degrees.

Cut the bread into halves lengthwise. Remove the bread centers, leaving the bread shells. Tear the bread centers into chunks.

Melt the butter in a skillet. Add the garlic and sesame seeds. Sauté until golden brown. Add the bread chunks. Fry until golden brown. Remove from the heat.

Mix the sour cream, Monterey Jack cheese, Parmesan cheese, parsley flakes and lemon pepper in a bowl. Add the artichoke hearts. Stir in the bread mixture. Spoon into the bread shells. Sprinkle with the Cheddar cheese.

Bake for 30 minutes. Remove from the oven. Garnish with tomato slices and parsley.

Hermit Cookies

4¹/2 cups flour
4 teaspoons baking soda
¹/2 teaspoon salt
2 teaspoons cinnamon
1¹/2 teaspoons ginger
1¹/2 teaspoons ground cloves
1 cup raisins

1 cup chopped nuts
2 cups sugar
1¹/2 cups (3 sticks) margarine, softened
2 eggs
¹/2 cup molasses
sugar for rolling

DIRECTIONS:

Mix the flour, baking soda, salt, cinnamon, ginger, cloves, raisins and nuts in
a bowl. Cream 2 cups sugar, margarine and eggs in a mixing bowl until light
and fluffy. Beat in the molasses. Add the flour mixture and mix well. Chill,
covered, for 2 hours.

Preheat the oven to 325 degrees.

Shape the dough into finger-size pieces. Roll in sugar. Arrange on greased
cookie sheets.

Bake for 7 minutes. Cool on wire racks.

Oreo Tailgate Fire Pie

SERVES 8

36 Oreo cookies
¹/4 cup (¹/2 stick) butter or margarine,
    melted

24 large marshmallows
¹/2 cup milk
1¹/2 cups whipping cream, whipped

DIRECTIONS:

Coarsely chop 10 of the cookies. Crush the remaining cookies to form fine
crumbs. Mix the cookie crumbs and butter in a bowl. Press evenly into a
9-inch pie plate. Chill in the refrigerator.

Cook the marshmallows and milk in a 2-quart saucepan over medium heat
until melted and smooth, stirring constantly. Remove from the heat to cool
completely. Fold in 2 cups of the whipped cream. Fold in the chopped
cookies. Spoon into the prepared pie plate. Chill for 4 hours or until firm.

Note: You may use whipped topping instead of whipped cream.

Mocha Sheet Cake

For a beautiful garnish, decorate
your dishes with edible flowers.

SERVES 36

2 cups flour
2 cups sugar
1 cup (2 sticks) margarine
1/4 cup baking cocoa
1 cup water
1/2 cup buttermilk

1 teaspoon baking soda
2 eggs, beaten
1/2 teaspoon vanilla extract
1/2 teaspoon cinnamon
Mocha Frosting (below)

DIRECTIONS:

Preheat the oven to 350 degrees.

Sift the flour and sugar into a large bowl. Bring the margarine, baking cocoa and water to a boil in a small saucepan. Pour over the flour mixture and stir by hand. Stir in a mixture of the buttermilk and baking soda. Add the eggs, vanilla and cinnamon and mix well. Pour into a buttered and floured 11×16-inch cake pan.

Bake for 20 minutes. Remove from the oven to cool slightly.

Spread Mocha Frosting over the warm cake.

Mocha Frosting

1/4 cup baking cocoa
1/2 cup (1 stick) butter or margarine
6 tablespoons brewed black coffee

1 (1-pound) package confectioners' sugar
1 teaspoon vanilla extract
1 cup chopped nuts

DIRECTIONS:

Bring the baking cocoa, butter and coffee to a boil in a saucepan, stirring constantly.

Add the confectioners' sugar and beat until smooth. Stir in the vanilla and nuts.

OKTOBERFEST

Looking for a reason to throw a party? Simply celebrate the month of October with this delicious fall fare.

Reuben Dip

SERVES 8 TO 10

8 ounces cream cheese, softened
1 cup sour cream
1 cup salsa
4 ounces corned beef, chopped

1/2 cup sauerkraut, drained and chopped
1 garlic clove, chopped
salt and pepper to taste

DIRECTIONS:

Preheat the oven to 350 degrees.

Beat the cream cheese, sour cream and salsa in a bowl until smooth. Stir in the corned beef, sauerkraut, garlic, salt and pepper.

Spoon into a shallow quiche dish.

Bake for 20 to 30 minutes or until bubbly.

Serve with crackers.

Whole Wheat Popovers

MAKES 6

1/2 cup whole wheat flour
1/2 cup all-purpose flour
1/4 teaspoon salt

3 eggs, beaten
1 cup milk
3 tablespoons vegetable oil

DIRECTIONS:

Preheat the oven to 375 degrees.

Mix the whole wheat flour, all-purpose flour and salt in a mixing bowl. Beat the eggs, milk and oil in a bowl. Add to the flour mixture and beat until smooth. Pour into 6 generously greased custard cups or medium muffin cups. Place on a baking sheet.

Bake for 45 to 50 minutes or until puffed and golden brown. Serve immediately with butter, honey or jam.

SERVES 6

1/4 cup (1/2 stick) butter
1 yellow onion, chopped
1/2 teaspoon ginger
1/2 teaspoon cinnamon
4 cups chicken stock or broth
1/2 cup dry sherry
2 medium butternut squash, peeled,
 seeded and chopped

1 1/2 apples, cored, peeled and chopped
1/2 cup whipping cream
salt and cayenne pepper to taste

Garnish:
chopped fresh chives

DIRECTIONS:

Melt the butter in a heavy Dutch oven over medium heat. Add the onion, ginger and cinnamon. Sauté until the onion is transparent. Add the stock, sherry, squash and apples.

Bring to a boil and reduce the heat. Simmer until the squash and apples are tender. Remove from the heat and cool slightly.

Purée in batches in a blender, pouring each batch into a large bowl after blending. Stir in the whipping cream, salt and cayenne pepper. Return to the Dutch oven.

Cook until heated through. Ladle into soup bowls. Garnish with chives.

Glazed Carrots

SERVES 2

1 tablespoon butter
1 tablespoon brown sugar
1/3 cup semidry white wine

1/3 cup water
1 cup fresh carrots, julienned

DIRECTIONS:

Melt the butter in a saucepan. Add the brown sugar, wine, water and carrots.

Bring to a boil and reduce the heat. Simmer, covered, for 15 to 20 minutes. Cook, uncovered, until the carrots are tender-crisp and most of the liquid has evaporated.

Roasted Mosaic Potatoes

SERVES 6

extra-virgin olive oil for brushing
1 1/2 pounds small new potatoes

sprigs of fresh herbs, such as rosemary,
    sage, oregano, thyme, chervil or
    Italian parsley
kosher salt

DIRECTIONS:

Preheat the oven to 375 degrees.

Line a baking sheet with parchment paper. Brush with olive oil.

Cut the potatoes into halves lengthwise. Arrange cut side up on the prepared baking sheet. Brush the potatoes with olive oil. Arrange herb sprigs atop each potato half, pressing lightly to adhere. Sprinkle with kosher salt.

Bake on the center oven rack for 15 minutes. Turn the potatoes. Bake for 15 to 20 minutes longer or until the potatoes are tender and golden brown.

To create "rose" garnishes, use a vegetable peeler to cut spirals of citrus zest or tomato skin. Once peeled, just twirl the zest or skin into a rose pattern.

Stuffed Pork Tenderloin with Blackberry Sauce

SERVES 4

1 (12-ounce) pork tenderloin, trimmed
1/2 cup cooked wild rice
1 tablespoon chopped red bell pepper
1 tablespoon chopped yellow bell pepper
1 tablespoon chopped green bell pepper
1 egg white
1/4 cup chopped onion
1 teaspoon minced garlic

dash of pepper
dash of marjoram
1 tablespoon honey
Blackberry Sauce (below)

Garnish:
fresh blackberries

DIRECTIONS:

Preheat the oven to 300 degrees.

Butterfly the pork. Combine the wild rice, bell peppers and egg white in a bowl and mix well.

Sauté the onion and garlic in a nonstick skillet until the onion is transparent. Add the rice mixture and mix well.

Cut 48 inches of cotton string into 6-inch pieces. Spread the string pieces evenly 1 inch apart. Lay the pork open face horizontally across the string. Fill the center of the pork with the rice mixture. Tie the ends of the pork together, beginning at 1 end. Arrange in a baking pan. Sprinkle with pepper and marjoram. Brush with the honey.

Bake, covered, for 45 minutes or until a meat thermometer inserted into the thickest portion registers 160 degrees.

To serve, remove from the oven and cool slightly. Cut into slices. Serve with Blackberry Sauce. Garnish with fresh blackberries.

Blackberry Sauce

1 cup blackberries
1/4 cup rich stock
1 tablespoon brandy or madeira
dash of garlic powder

1 tablespoon sugar
1 tablespoon raspberry vinegar
1 tablespoon cornstarch
1 tablespoon cold water

DIRECTIONS:

Purée the blackberries in a blender until smooth. Strain into a saucepan, discarding the seeds.

Heat over low heat. Add the stock, brandy and garlic powder and mix well.

Caramelize the sugar in the vinegar in a saucepan over high heat, stirring constantly. Add to the blackberry mixture and mix well. Mix the cornstarch and cold water in a bowl. Add to the sauce.

Bring to a boil. Cook until thickened, stirring constantly.

PHOTOGRAPH RIGHT

Swiss Apple Pie

1 cup sugar
1/4 cup (1/2 stick) butter, melted
1 egg
1 teaspoon baking soda
2 teaspoons hot water
1 cup flour
1 teaspoon cinnamon

1/4 teaspoon cloves
1/4 teaspoon allspice
1 teaspoon nutmeg
2 1/2 cups chopped Granny Smith apples
1/2 cup chopped nuts
Rum Sauce (below)

DIRECTIONS:

Preheat the oven to 350 degrees.

Combine the sugar and butter in a mixing bowl and mix well. Beat in the egg. Dissolve the baking soda in the hot water in a bowl. Stir into the egg mixture. Add the flour, cinnamon, cloves, allspice and nutmeg and mix well. Stir in the apples and nuts. (The batter will be thick.) Spoon into a greased 9-inch pie plate.

Bake for 50 to 60 minutes or until golden brown. Serve with Rum Sauce.

Rum Sauce

1/2 cup sugar
1/2 cup packed brown sugar
1/2 cup cream

1 teaspoon white corn syrup
1/2 teaspoon vanilla extract
1/2 teaspoon rum flavoring

DIRECTIONS:

Bring the sugar, brown sugar, cream and corn syrup to a boil in a saucepan. Boil for 30 seconds, stirring constantly. Remove from the heat.

Beat until cool. Add the vanilla and rum flavoring.

Reheat before serving.

TEXAS TUSCAN

Treat your guests to a Tuscan meal with Texas flair. You will find that the flavors of these two cultures—both with long, proud traditions—complement each other beautifully.

Caponata

SERVES 6 TO 8

1¹/3 cups vegetable oil
1 cup chopped onion
1/2 cup sliced celery
1/2 cup red bell pepper
1/2 cup yellow bell pepper
4 zucchini, chopped

2 cups chopped tomatoes
2 tablespoons chopped fresh basil
2 tablespoons lemon juice
1/2 cup sliced olives
2 tablespoons capers
salt and pepper to taste

DIRECTIONS:

Heat the oil in a skillet. Add the onion, celery and bell peppers. Sauté until the onion is translucent. Add the zucchini, tomatoes and basil.

Bring to a boil and reduce the heat. Simmer for 15 minutes. Remove from the heat.

Add the lemon juice, olives and capers and mix well. Season with salt and pepper. Spoon into a bowl.

Chill, covered, until ready to serve. Serve with pita chips or focaccia.

Bruschetta

Add a couple of paper towels to your salad spinner to quickly and thoroughly dry lettuce for salads.

SERVES 6 TO 8

1 French baguette
3 ripe tomatoes, peeled and chopped
4 garlic cloves, minced

1 to 2 tablespoons olive oil
1 tablespoon balsamic vinegar
salt and freshly ground pepper to taste

DIRECTIONS:

Preheat the oven to 325 degrees.
    Cut the baguette into slices 1/4 inch thick. Arrange on a baking sheet.
    Bake until lightly toasted. Do not brown.
    Mix the tomatoes, garlic, olive oil, vinegar, salt and pepper in a bowl.
Marinate at room temperature for 1 to 2 hours.
    Spread over the baguette slices to serve.

Italian Salad

SERVES 4 TO 6

5 tablespoons olive oil
1 tablespoon red wine vinegar
4 ounces Gorgonzola cheese, crumbled

salt and pepper to taste
1/2 cup coarsely chopped walnuts
1 head romaine or Bibb lettuce, torn

DIRECTIONS:

Combine the olive oil, vinegar and 1/2 of the cheese in a bowl and mash well.
Season with salt and pepper. Stir in 1/2 of the walnuts.
    Arrange the romaine on salad plates. Drizzle with the dressing. Sprinkle
with the remaining cheese and walnuts.

Chicken Piccata

SERVES 4

1 pound boneless chicken tenders
salt and pepper to taste
flour for dredging
1/2 cup (1 stick) margarine
3 green onions, chopped
2 garlic cloves, minced
8 ounces fresh mushrooms, sliced

1 chicken bouillon cube
juice of 1 lemon
3/4 cup water
1/2 cup white wine
1 tablespoon chopped fresh parsley, or
   1 teaspoon dried parsley
grated Parmesan cheese (optional)

DIRECTIONS:

Season the chicken with salt and pepper. Dredge in the flour. Sauté in the margarine in a skillet until light brown. Remove the chicken to a plate.

Sauté the green onions and garlic in the drippings in the skillet for 2 minutes. Add the mushrooms, bouillon cube, lemon juice, water and wine and mix well. Return the chicken to the skillet.

Bring to a boil and reduce the heat. Simmer for 15 minutes, adding liquid if needed. Sprinkle with the parsley and cheese just before serving.

Pasta with Tomato, Basil and Crisp Bread Crumbs

SERVES 8

1 cup coarsely chopped whole wheat
   bread crumbs
6 tablespoons extra-virgin olive oil
salt and freshly ground pepper to taste
4 ounces balsamic vinegar
2 cups yellow cherry tomato halves

2 cups red cherry tomato halves
16 ounces fresh pasta, such as linguini,
   angel hair or fettuccini
coarsely shredded fresh Parmigiano-
   Reggiano cheese
1 bunch fresh basil leaves, cut in a
   chiffonade

DIRECTIONS:

Preheat the oven to 375 degrees.

Toss the bread crumbs, 2 tablespoons of the olive oil, salt and pepper in a bowl. Spread on a baking sheet. Bake for 8 to 10 minutes or until toasted, turning occasionally. Remove from the oven to cool.

Blend the remaining 4 tablespoons olive oil, vinegar, salt and pepper in a bowl using a hand-held blender. Add the yellow and red cherry tomatoes and toss to coat. Cover with plastic wrap.

Cook the pasta in boiling water in a saucepan until al dente; drain. Add the tomato mixture and bread crumbs and toss to mix well. Spoon into a large pasta bowl. Sprinkle with the cheese and basil.

Note: You may also add grilled chicken or shrimp.

Penne in Cream Sauce with Sausage

When cooking pasta, add a tablespoon of butter or cooking oil to the saucepan of boiling water to keep the pasta from boiling over.

SERVES 6 TO 8

1 tablespoon butter
1 tablespoon olive oil
1 medium onion, thinly sliced
3 garlic cloves, minced
1 pound sweet Italian sausage, casings removed
2/3 cup dry white wine
1 (14-ounce) can diced peeled tomatoes

1 cup whipping cream
1/4 cup chopped fresh Italian parsley
salt and pepper to taste
16 ounces penne
1 cup freshly grated Parmesan cheese
2 tablespoons chopped fresh Italian parsley

DIRECTIONS:

Melt the butter in the olive oil in a heavy skillet over medium-high heat. Add the onion and garlic. Sauté for 7 minutes or until golden brown and tender. Add the sausage. Sauté for 7 minutes or until golden brown and crumbly; drain. Stir in the wine.

Boil for 2 minutes or until almost all of the liquid evaporates. Add the undrained tomatoes. Simmer for 3 minutes. Add the cream. Simmer for 5 minutes or until the sauce thickens slightly. Stir in 1/4 cup parsley. Season with salt and pepper. Remove from the heat. (You may prepare 1 day ahead and chill, covered, in the refrigerator.)

Cook the pasta in boiling salted water in a large saucepan until al dente; drain. Place in a large serving bowl. Return the sauce to a simmer. Pour over the pasta. Add 3/4 cup of the cheese and toss to coat. Sprinkle with the remaining 1/4 cup cheese and 2 tablespoons parsley.

Herb Bread Swizzle Sticks

MAKES 2 DOZEN

1/4 cup grated Parmesan cheese
1/2 teaspoon basil leaves, crushed
1/2 teaspoon oregano leaves, crushed
1/4 teaspoon pepper

1 egg white
1 tablespoon water
1 (12-count) package refrigerated
  breadstick dough

DIRECTIONS:

Preheat the oven to 350 degrees.

Mix the cheese, basil, oregano and pepper in a small bowl. Beat the egg white and water in a small bowl.

Separate the breadstick dough on a piece of waxed paper. Cut each lengthwise into halves. Sprinkle with 2/3 of the cheese mixture; roll each to coat and twist. Arrange on 2 baking sheets sprayed with nonstick cooking spray. Brush lightly with the egg white mixture. Sprinkle with the Parmesan cheese mixture.

Bake for 15 minutes or until light brown.

Olive Cheese Bread

MAKES 1½ DOZEN

3 cups baking mix
1 cup milk
1/3 cup butter, softened
1 tablespoon dry onion flakes
1 teaspoon Worcestershire sauce
1/8 teaspoon Tabasco sauce

2 cups (8 ounces) shredded Monterey Jack
  cheese
1 cup sliced black olives
1 egg, lightly beaten
1 teaspoon Italian seasoning

DIRECTIONS:

Preheat the oven to 425 degrees.

Combine the baking mix and milk in a bowl and mix well. Spread in a greased 14-inch pizza pan. Combine the butter, onion flakes, Worcestershire sauce, Tabasco sauce, cheese, olives, egg and Italian seasoning in a bowl and mix well. Spread over the dough.

Bake for 20 to 25 minutes or until golden brown. Cut into wedges and serve.

Berry Tiramisu

1 1/2 cups raspberries
1 cup blueberries
1 cup strawberries, cut into quarters
2 tablespoons sugar
1/2 cup plus 3 tablespoons Chambord or
    other raspberry-flavored liqueur
Raspberry Coulis (page 119)
2 cups whipping cream

1/4 cup confectioners' sugar
1 pound mascarpone cheese
1/4 cup confectioners' sugar
8 (1/2-inch-thick) slices pound cake

Garnish:
sprigs of fresh mint

DIRECTIONS:

Combine the raspberries, blueberries and strawberries, sugar, 2 tablespoons of the Chambord and 1/2 cup of the Raspberry Coulis in a bowl and toss to mix.

Whip the cream in a mixing bowl at high speed until almost doubled in volume. Add 1/4 cup confectioners' sugar and 1 tablespoon of the remaining Chambord. Whip until stiff peaks form.

Whip the cheese with 1/4 cup confectioners' sugar in a mixing bowl at low speed until smooth. Fold in 1/2 of the whipped cream mixture.

Arrange 1/2 of the cake in a 6×9-inch pan. Drizzle 1/4 cup of the remaining Chambord over the cake. Cover with 1/2 of the berry mixture. Spread 1/2 of the cheese mixture and remaining whipped cream mixture over the berries, gently spreading into a smooth layer. Repeat the layers with the remaining ingredients. Cover tightly with plastic wrap.

Chill for 2 hours or up to 1 1/2 days. Spoon into serving bowls. Garnish with mint. Serve with the remaining Raspberry Coulis spooned over each serving or pass on the side.

Raspberry Coulis

2 cups raspberries (about 12 ounces)
3/4 cup Simple Syrup (below)
1 1/2 tablespoons fresh lemon juice

1/2 tablespoon cornstarch
2 teaspoons cold water

For a beautiful glass of water, freeze one edible flower in each section of an ice cube tray. Once the cubes are frozen, fill your guests' glasses with the ice and add water.

DIRECTIONS:

Bring the raspberries, Simple Syrup and lemon juice to a simmer in a medium saucepan over low heat. Simmer for 10 minutes or until the berries are very soft, stirring occasionally. Sprinkle the cornstarch over the cold water in a bowl and stir to dissolve. Add to the raspberry mixture.

Cook for 3 minutes or until the sauce thickens, stirring occasionally. Strain through a fine-mesh wire sieve into a medium bowl, discarding the seeds. Cool completely. Chill, covered, until ready to use.

Note: You may freeze any leftover Raspberry Coulis in a plastic container for up to 1 month.

Simple Syrup

MAKES 4 CUPS

2 cups sugar

2 cups water

DIRECTIONS:

Bring the sugar and water to a boil in a heavy medium saucepan over high heat. Reduce the heat to medium-low. Simmer for 6 to 8 minutes or until the sugar is completely dissolved, stirring constantly. Remove from the heat to cool completely.

Pour into an airtight container. Chill, covered, for 4 hours before using.

Gelato Siciliano

Just before your guests arrive, spray a mixture of water and a few drops of vanilla extract around the house. When mixing, add the extract slowly—a little bit goes a long way.

4 cups milk
1 cup sugar
3 tablespoons cornstarch

2 cups shelled unsalted pistachios,
    finely ground

DIRECTIONS:

Bring 3 cups of the milk to a simmer in a medium saucepan over medium heat. Remove from the heat.

Blend the remaining 1 cup milk, sugar and cornstarch in a bowl. Stir into the hot milk.

Return to the heat. Cook for 8 to 10 minutes or until slightly thickened, stirring constantly. Place the pistachios in a bowl. Stir in the hot mixture.

Let stand until cool. Cover with plastic wrap. Chill for 8 to 12 hours.

Strain the mixture through a fine sieve into an ice cream freezer, pressing the pistachios with the back of a wooden spoon. Discard the pistachios. Freeze using the manufacturer's directions.

Chocolate Gelato

SERVES 4

3 cups milk
3/4 cup sugar

2 tablespoons cornstarch
3/4 cup baking cocoa

DIRECTIONS:

Simmer 2 cups of the milk in a medium saucepan over medium heat and remove from the heat. Mix the remaining 1 cup milk, sugar, cornstarch and baking cocoa in a bowl and stir into the hot milk. Cook until the sugar and cornstarch dissolve.

Let stand until cool. Cover with plastic wrap. Chill for 8 to 12 hours. Pour into an ice cream freezer. Freeze using the manufacturer's directions.

PUMPKIN SUPPER

Serve your guests a unique menu of soups and breads. After dinner, continue with the theme by holding a pumpkin carving contest!

Spicy Pumpkin Dip

MAKES 3 CUPS

1¹/2 cups canned pumpkin purée
1¹/2 cups canned chick-peas, rinsed
    and drained
3 tablespoons tahini (sesame paste)
1 garlic clove

1 teaspoon cayenne pepper
1 teaspoon cumin
2 tablespoons olive oil
2 tablespoons lemon juice
salt and pepper to taste

DIRECTIONS:

Process the pumpkin and chick-peas in a food processor until nearly smooth. Add the tahini, garlic, cayenne pepper, cumin, olive oil, lemon juice, salt and pepper and process until smooth. Adjust the seasonings to taste.

Serve with pita chips.

Bacon-Stuffed Tomatoes

MAKES 3 CUPS FILLING

16 ounces cream cheese, softened
1 (10-ounce) can tomatoes with
    green chiles
chopped green onions to taste
bacon bits to taste

cherry tomatoes

Garnish:
chopped fresh cilantro

DIRECTIONS:

Combine the cream cheese, tomatoes with green chiles, green onions and bacon bits in a bowl and mix well. Chill, covered, until firm.

Scoop out the centers from the tomatoes. Fill with the bacon mixture. Garnish with cilantro.

Note: Do not use real bacon chips in this recipe. You may serve any leftover bacon mixture as a dip with bagel chips or crackers.

Menu

SPICY PUMPKIN DIP

BACON-STUFFED
TOMATOES

SOUR CREAM CHEDDAR
BISCUITS

CHEDDAR CHOWDER

POTATO CHEESE SOUP

BEST-KEPT-SECRET
SOUP

STEW IN A PUMPKIN

HALLOWEEN PUMPKIN
COOKIES

DREAMY HIGH
PUMPKIN PIE

Sour Cream Cheddar Biscuits

Cheeses should always be served at room temperature (about seventy degrees).

MAKES 2 DOZEN

1/2 cup (1 stick) butter, melted
1/2 cup light sour cream

1/2 cup (2 ounces) shredded Cheddar cheese
1 cup self-rising flour

DIRECTIONS:

Preheat the oven to 400 degrees.

Combine the butter, sour cream and cheese in a bowl. Stir in the self-rising flour. Drop by rounded teaspoonfuls into ungreased miniature muffin cups.

Bake for 15 minutes or until light golden brown. Remove from the muffin cups immediately.

Note: You may also drop the batter by teaspoonfuls onto an ungreased baking sheet.

Cheddar Chowder

SERVES 8

2 cups boiling water
2 cups cauliflower florets
1 cup chopped potatoes
1/2 cup sliced carrots
1/2 cup sliced celery
1/4 cup chopped onion

1 1/2 teaspoons salt
1/4 teaspoon pepper
1/4 cup (1/2 stick) margarine
1/4 cup flour
2 cups milk
2 cups (8 ounces) shredded Cheddar cheese

DIRECTIONS:

Combine the water, cauliflower, potatoes, carrots, celery, onion, salt and pepper in a saucepan. Simmer, covered, for 10 minutes.

Melt the margarine in a large saucepan. Stir in the flour. Add the milk gradually, stirring constantly. Bring to a boil. Cook until thickened, stirring constantly. Add the cheese. Cook until melted, stirring constantly. Add the undrained vegetables. Cook until heated through. Do not boil.

Potato Cheese Soup

3 medium potatoes
salt to taste
1 cup water
1/4 cup finely chopped onion
milk
3 tablespoons butter, melted

2 tablespoons flour
2 tablespoons snipped fresh parsley
3/4 teaspoon salt
freshly ground pepper to taste
1 cup (4 ounces) shredded Swiss cheese

DIRECTIONS:

Peel the potatoes and cut into pieces. Bring the salted water to a boil in a
2-quart saucepan. Add the potatoes and onion.

Cook, covered, for 20 minutes or until tender. Mash slightly; do not drain.
Pour into a liquid measure. Add enough milk to measure 5 cups. Return to
the saucepan.

Mix the butter, flour, parsley, 3/4 teaspoon salt and pepper in a bowl. Stir
into the potato mixture.

Cook until thickened and bubbly, stirring constantly. Add the cheese.
Cook until the cheese is partially melted, stirring constantly.

Ladle into soup bowls and serve immediately.

Best-Kept-Secret Soup

Never use strongly scented flowers or candles in your dining room. The scents mixed with the aromas of your food will overwhelm your guests.

SERVES 8

1 (15-ounce) can chili
1 (11-ounce) can Shoe Peg corn
1 (10-ounce) can vegetable beef soup
1 (10-ounce) can tomato soup

1 (10-ounce) can tomatoes with green chiles
1 (14-ounce) can stewed tomatoes
1 package corn chips

DIRECTIONS:

Combine the chili, corn, canned soups, tomatoes with green chiles and stewed tomatoes in a saucepan and mix well.

Cook until heated through, stirring constantly.

Place the corn chips in each serving bowl. Ladle the soup over the chips.

Note: You may add one 4-ounce can green chiles.

Stew in a Pumpkin

SERVES 6

2 pounds lean ground beef
1 cup chopped potatoes
1 cup chopped celery
1 cup chopped carrots
1 cup chopped onions
2 tablespoons Worcestershire sauce
lemon pepper marinade to taste

salt and pepper to taste
2 tablespoons tapioca
3 (5.5-ounce) cans tomato juice cocktail
   or canned tomato juice
1 medium well-formed pumpkin
1/2 cup milk

DIRECTIONS:

Preheat the oven to 250 degrees.

Combine the ground beef, potatoes, celery, carrots, onions, Worcestershire sauce, lemon pepper marinade, salt and pepper in an ovenproof baking dish and mix well. Dissolve the tapioca in the tomato juice cocktail in a bowl. Pour over the ground beef mixture.

Bake for 5 hours. Do not peek.

Increase the oven temperature to 350 degrees.

Cut the top from the pumpkin and reserve. Scoop out the seeds and loose pulp from the pumpkin and discard. Rinse the inside of the pumpkin with the milk. Sprinkle with salt and pepper. Replace the top. Place on a baking sheet.

Bake for 45 to 60 minutes.

Ladle the hot stew into the pumpkin. To serve, ladle the stew into soup bowls, scooping out a little pumpkin pulp with each serving.

Halloween Pumpkin Cookies

MAKES 50

2¹/4 cups flour
¹/4 teaspoon cinnamon
¹/4 teaspoon ginger
¹/4 teaspoon nutmeg
pinch of salt
³/4 cup (1¹/2 sticks) butter, softened

¹/2 cup packed light brown sugar
2 or 3 tablespoons finely grated
  orange zest
¹/2 cup canned pumpkin
1 egg yolk, beaten
Decorator Icing (below)

DIRECTIONS:

Sift the flour, cinnamon, ginger, nutmeg and salt into a large bowl.

Cream the butter, brown sugar and orange zest in a mixing bowl until soft and pale yellow. Add to the flour mixture with the pumpkin and egg yolk and mix to form a soft dough. Wrap in plastic wrap. Chill for 30 minutes.

Preheat the oven to 375 degrees.

Divide the dough into 2 equal portions. Roll each portion 1/8 inch thick on a lightly floured surface. Cut with Halloween-shaped cookie cutters, such as cats, pumpkins and owls, rerolling the trimmings as necessary. Arrange on greased cookie sheets.

Bake for 10 to 15 minutes or until light golden brown. Remove to wire racks to cool.

Drizzle or pipe Decorator Icing on the cooled cookies in patterns of choice. Store in airtight containers.

Decorator Icing

MAKES 4 CUPS

4 cups packed confectioners' sugar
4 egg whites
1 teaspoon fresh lemon juice

orange food coloring
black food coloring

DIRECTIONS:

Sift the confectioners' sugar into a medium bowl. Add the egg whites and lemon juice and mix until smooth. Spoon 1/2 of the mixture into a separate bowl. Tint 1/2 of the mixture orange and the remaining portion black.

Note: To avoid raw eggs that may carry salmonella, we suggest using an equivalent amount of pasteurized egg substitute.

Dreamy High Pumpkin Pie

2/3 cup sugar
1 envelope unflavored gelatin
1 teaspoon cinnamon
1/2 teaspoon salt
1/4 teaspoon nutmeg
3 egg yolks, lightly beaten
3/4 cup milk

1 cup cooked pumpkin
3 egg whites
1/3 cup sugar
1 (9-inch) graham cracker pie shell
1/2 cup whipping cream, whipped
1/2 cup flaked coconut, toasted

DIRECTIONS:

Combine 2/3 cup sugar, unflavored gelatin, cinnamon, salt and nutmeg in a large saucepan and mix well. Beat the egg yolks and milk in a bowl. Add to the gelatin mixture.

Cook until slightly thickened, stirring constantly. Stir in the pumpkin. Chill until the mixture mounds slightly when dropped from a spoon, stirring frequently.

Beat the egg whites in a mixing bowl until soft peaks form. Add 1/3 cup sugar gradually, beating until stiff peaks form. Fold in the chilled pumpkin mixture. Spoon into the pie shell.

Chill until firm. Dollop the top with the whipped cream. Sprinkle with the toasted coconut.

ELEGANT DINNER PARTY

When you wish to treat your guests to an event, serve this menu. Your guests are sure to remember it for years to come. If you prefer to lighten the flavor a bit, simply serve the dressing and sauce on the side.

Apple, Endive and Parmesan Salad with Walnut Vinaigrette

SERVES 6

2 tablespoons orange juice
2 teaspoons Dijon mustard
1/4 cup olive oil
2 tablespoons walnut oil
salt and pepper to taste
2 Red Delicious apples, unpeeled and
   thinly sliced

2 tablespoons orange juice
4 heads Belgian endive
1 head butter lettuce, torn into bite-size
   pieces
3/4 cup walnuts, toasted and chopped
2 tablespoons chopped fresh chives
Parmesan cheese shavings

DIRECTIONS:

Whisk 2 tablespoons orange juice and the Dijon mustard in a small bowl until blended. Whisk in the olive oil and walnut oil. Season with salt and pepper.

Toss the apples in 2 tablespoons orange juice in a large bowl.

Separate the endive leaves, reserving 24 leaves. Cut the remaining leaves into slices. Add the sliced endive, butter lettuce and walnuts to the apples. Add the vinaigrette and toss to coat.

Arrange 4 reserved endive leaves in spoke fashion on each of 6 salad plates. Mound the salad atop the endive leaves. Sprinkle with the chives. Top each with Parmesan cheese shavings.

Brie Soup

SERVES 6

1 (12-ounce) wheel Brie cheese,
    at room temperature
3 tablespoons butter
2 carrots, thinly sliced
2 ribs celery, thinly sliced
2 green onions, thinly sliced

8 mushrooms, thinly sliced
1/2 cup flour
3 (16-ounce) cans Healthy Request
    chicken broth
1/2 cup milk
pepper to taste

DIRECTIONS:

Remove the rind from the cheese and discard. Cut the cheese into cubes.

Melt the butter in a large saucepan. Add the carrots and celery. Sauté for 3 to 4 minutes. Add the green onions and mushrooms. Cook until soft and light brown. Stir in the flour. Pour into a large stockpot. Add the broth.

Bring to a boil. Cook for 5 minutes. Remove from the heat. Add the cheese and stir to mix well.

Cook over low heat until blended. Stir in the milk. Season with pepper.

Garlic Croutons

MAKES 2 CUPS

3 or 4 garlic cloves, minced
1/4 cup olive oil

2 cups cubed French bread
grated Romano or Parmesan cheese

DIRECTIONS:

Preheat the oven to 300 degrees.

Sauté the garlic in the olive oil in a skillet. Add the bread. Sauté until golden brown. Arrange the bread in a single layer on a baking sheet. Sprinkle with cheese.

Bake for 15 minutes or until crisp. Serve with soup, salad or vegetables.

Elegant Almond Broccoli in Sherry Sauce

SERVES 6

1 1/2 pounds broccoli, trimmed and
    separated into florets
4 cups boiling water
1 chicken bouillon cube
1 cup boiling water
1/3 cup butter
1/3 cup flour

1 1/2 cups half-and-half
3 tablespoons sherry
2 tablespoons lemon juice
1/2 teaspoon salt
1/4 teaspoon pepper
3/4 cup shredded Parmesan cheese
1/2 cup slivered almonds, toasted

DIRECTIONS:

Preheat the oven to 375 degrees.

Cook the broccoli in 4 cups boiling water in a saucepan over medium heat for 4 to 5 minutes or until tender-crisp; drain. Arrange in a lightly greased 2-quart baking dish.

Dissolve the bouillon cube in 1 cup boiling water in a bowl.

Melt the butter in a large saucepan over medium-high heat. Whisk in the flour. Cook for 1 minute, whisking constantly. Whisk in the bouillon mixture and half-and-half gradually. Cook until the mixture thickens and comes to a boil, stirring constantly.

Whisk in the sherry, lemon juice, salt and pepper. Pour over the broccoli. Sprinkle with the cheese and almonds.

Bake for 20 minutes or until bubbly.

For a special touch, use a small cookie cutter or a floral or shell mold to cut individual pats of butter for your guests.

Mushroom Mousse

Slice the mushrooms quickly and perfectly by using an egg slicer.

SERVES 10 TO 12

2 pounds mushrooms, finely chopped
4 cups whipping cream
10 eggs
5 egg yolks

5 shallots, sliced
1/8 teaspoon nutmeg
salt and pepper to taste

DIRECTIONS:

Preheat the oven to 350 degrees.

Process the mushrooms, whipping cream, eggs, egg yolks, shallots, nutmeg, salt and pepper in a food processor until smooth. Reserve 1 cup of the mixture to use for the sauce.

Pour the remaining mixture into a greased baking dish. Place the dish in a larger pan. Fill the larger pan with enough water to come halfway up the side of the baking dish.

Bake for 20 minutes or until a knife inserted in the center comes out clean.

Cook the reserved mixture in a saucepan over medium heat until slightly thickened, whisking constantly. Serve over the mousse.

Bell Peppers with Garlic and Basil

SERVES 6

6 yellow bell peppers
6 tablespoons extra-virgin olive oil
3 garlic cloves, finely chopped

salt and pepper to taste
handful of fresh basil leaves

DIRECTIONS:

Preheat the oven to 350 degrees.

Cut the bell peppers into halves and discard the seeds and fibers. Arrange cut side up on a baking sheet. Brush with some of the olive oil. Sprinkle with the garlic.

Bake for 40 minutes. Season with salt and pepper.

Arrange the baked bell peppers on a platter. Sprinkle with salt. Brush with the remaining olive oil. Shred the basil and sprinkle over the top.

Basil-Crusted Veal Chops

SERVES 2

1/4 cup minced fresh basil
1/4 cup fresh bread crumbs
1/4 cup packed freshly grated Parmesan
    cheese
2 tablespoons butter, softened
2 teaspoons coarse-grain mustard

salt and pepper to taste
2 (8-ounce) veal loin chops
    (about 1 1/2 inches thick)
1 tablespoon olive oil
2 tablespoons fresh bread crumbs

DIRECTIONS:

Preheat the oven to 450 degrees.

Mix the basil, 1/4 cup bread crumbs, cheese, butter and mustard in a small bowl. Season with salt and pepper.

Pat the veal chops dry with paper towels. Sprinkle with salt and pepper. Heat the olive oil in a large heavy ovenproof skillet over high heat. Add the veal. Cook for 1 minute on each side or until brown. Remove from the heat. Press the basil mixture on the top of each veal chop. Sprinkle with 2 tablespoons bread crumbs.

Bake for 15 minutes for medium-rare.

Note: Use bread crumbs made from crustless French bread.

Poppy Seed Crescent Rolls

SERVES 16

1/2 cup (1 stick) butter, softened
3 tablespoons dried minced onion

3 tablespoons poppy seeds
2 (8-count) cans crescent rolls

DIRECTIONS:

Preheat the oven to 375 degrees.

Mash the butter in a bowl with a spoon. Add the onion and poppy seeds and mix to form a paste.

Unroll the crescent roll dough. Separate into 16 triangles. Spread each with the poppy seed paste and roll up. Arrange on a baking sheet.

Bake for 11 to 14 minutes or until brown.

Chocolate-Crusted Crème Brûlée

SERVES 8

4¹/2 ounces semisweet chocolate
¹/4 cup (¹/2 stick) unsalted butter
¹/2 cup sugar
¹/2 teaspoon vanilla extract
¹/4 teaspoon salt
1 egg
¹/4 cup flour

³/4 cup pecans
3 cups whipping cream
¹/2 vanilla bean, split into halves
   lengthwise
6 egg yolks
6 tablespoons plus 8 teaspoons sugar

DIRECTIONS:

Preheat the oven to 350 degrees.

Melt the chocolate and butter in a saucepan over low heat, stirring constantly. Pour into a large bowl. Cool for 10 minutes.

Whisk ¹/2 cup sugar, ¹/2 teaspoon vanilla and salt into the chocolate mixture. Whisk in 1 egg. Add the flour and mix well. Stir in the pecans. Pour into a greased and floured 8×8 inch baking pan.

Bake for 20 minutes or until set. Cool and cut into 8 squares.

Pour the cream into a medium saucepan. Scrape the seeds from the vanilla bean into the cream with the bean. Bring to a simmer and remove from the heat. Discard the bean.

Whisk 6 egg yolks and 6 tablespoons sugar in a large bowl. Whisk a small amount of the hot mixture into the egg yolks. Whisk the egg yolks into the hot mixture. Cook over low heat for 2 minutes. Pour through a fine strainer into a bowl.

Reduce the oven temperature to 325 degrees.

Press 1 chocolate square on the bottom of each of eight ³/4-cup custard cups. Add the custard mixture. Arrange the cups in a large baking pan. Add enough hot water to the larger pan to come halfway up the side of the custard cups. Cover with foil.

Bake for 35 minutes or until set. Cool on wire racks. Chill for 3 hours.

Preheat the broiler.

Arrange the custard cups on a heavy baking sheet. Sprinkle each with 1 teaspoon of sugar.

Broil for 2 minutes. Chill for 3 to 6 hours before serving.

ELECTION DAY PARTY

Serve a simple but delicious dinner as you watch the results come in on election day. Select one of the two main courses for a small party—or serve both if you have a large guest list.

Pesto Brie

SERVES 6 TO 8

1 (1-pound) wheel Brie cheese
1 plum tomato, seeded and chopped
2 green onions, thinly sliced

1/4 cup prepared pesto
1 loaf French bread, sliced and toasted

DIRECTIONS:

Preheat the oven to 350 degrees.

Trim the rind from the cheese and discard. Cut the cheese into chunks. Layer the cheese, tomato and green onions in a baking dish. Dot with the pesto.

Bake until the cheese melts and the pesto begins to run.

Serve warm with the bread slices.

Mixed Greens with Balsamic Vinaigrette

SERVES 4

1 large shallot
1/4 cup hot water
2 tablespoons balsamic vinegar
1 1/2 tablespoons extra-virgin olive oil or
    walnut oil
1 tablespoon chopped fresh basil, or
    1 teaspoon dried basil

freshly ground pepper to taste
1 tablespoon crumbled bleu cheese
    (1/4 ounce) (optional)
4 cups mixed field greens or spinach
1/2 cup finely sliced red onions

DIRECTIONS:

Process the shallot, water, vinegar, olive oil, basil and pepper in a food processor or blender until smooth. Stir in the cheese. (You may chill, covered, for up to 5 days.)

Combine the mixed field greens and red onions in a salad bowl and toss to mix. Add the vinaigrette and toss to coat.

Grilled Shrimp with Firecracker Sauce

1 teaspoon fresh gingerroot, peeled and
  minced
1 medium tomato, cut into halves
1 medium red bell pepper, seeded
1 teaspoon garlic, minced
2 teaspoons Szechuan red chile sauce

1/4 cup sugar
2 tablespoons rice wine vinegar
2 teaspoons cornstarch
1/2 cup water
24 jumbo shrimp, peeled and deveined
hot cooked rice

DIRECTIONS:

Process the gingerroot, tomato, bell pepper, garlic, red chile sauce, sugar and
vinegar in a food processor until smooth. Pour into a small saucepan.

Bring to a boil. Dissolve the cornstarch in the water in a cup. Whisk into
the tomato mixture. Return to a boil. Boil for 1 minute, whisking constantly.
(The sauce may be made up to 1 day ahead, refrigerated and heated
before serving.)

Preheat the grill.

Thread 6 shrimp on four 6-inch skewers.

Grill for 4 minutes on each side or until the shrimp turn pink. Remove
the shrimp from the skewers.

To serve, arrange the shrimp on a bed of hot cooked rice. Spoon the sauce
over the shrimp. Serve immediately.

Creole Gumbo

SERVES 6 TO 8

For a lovely fall centerpiece, fill a large wooden or pottery bowl with gourds, squash, and Indian corn.

1 whole frying chicken, cut up
vegetable oil for frying
4 cups water
1/4 cup vegetable oil
2 tablespoons flour
1 cup chopped celery
1 onion, chopped
3 garlic cloves, minced
6 inches smoked sausage, thinly sliced
1 (14-ounce) can whole tomatoes, coarsely
    chopped

2 (10-ounce) packages frozen cut okra
2 tablespoons parsley flakes
1 bay leaf
1/4 teaspoon thyme
1/4 teaspoon Tabasco sauce, or to taste
salt to taste
1 pound fresh shrimp
1 1/4 pints (20 fluid ounces) fresh oysters
3 uncooked crab claw clusters
hot cooked rice
gumbo filé

DIRECTIONS:

Fry the chicken in oil in a skillet until partially cooked; drain. Arrange the chicken in a large saucepan. Add the water. Boil until tender and cooked through. Drain, reserving 3 cups of the broth. Chop the chicken coarsely, discarding the skin and bones.

Heat 1/4 cup oil in a stockpot or Dutch oven over low heat. Add the flour. Cook until the roux is dark brown, stirring constantly. Add the celery, onion, garlic and sausage. Cook until tender, stirring constantly. Add the tomatoes, okra, parsley flakes, bay leaf, thyme, Tabasco sauce and salt.

Simmer, covered, for 45 minutes. Add the chicken, shrimp, oysters and crab. Adjust the seasonings. Simmer for 10 minutes or until the shrimp turn pink and the edges of the oysters curl. Discard the bay leaf.

Ladle over hot rice in large flat serving bowls. Sprinkle with gumbo filé.

PHOTOGRAPH ON PAGE 136

Kahlúa Cake

1 (2-layer) package yellow cake mix
1 (4-ounce) package vanilla instant
    pudding mix
1 cup vegetable oil
3/4 cup water
4 eggs

1/4 cup Kahlúa
1/4 cup vodka
1 cup sugar
1 tablespoon butter
1/4 cup water
2 tablespoons Kahlúa
2 tablespoons vodka

DIRECTIONS:

Preheat the oven to 350 degrees.

Combine the cake mix and pudding mix in a mixing bowl and mix well. Add the oil, 3/4 cup water, eggs, 1/4 cup Kahlúa and 1/4 cup vodka. Beat for 4 to 5 minutes. Pour into a greased and floured bundt pan.

Bake for 55 to 60 minutes or until a cake tester inserted in the center comes out clean. Remove the pan to a wire rack.

Bring the sugar, butter and 1/4 cup water to a boil in a saucepan. Boil for 1 minute. Remove from the heat. Stir in 2 tablespoons Kahlúa and 2 tablespoons vodka. Pour gradually over the hot cake. Let the cake cool for at least 1 hour before inverting and removing from the pan.

Lemon Cream Cheese Cake

SERVES 8 TO 12

1/2 cup (1 stick) butter, softened
1 (2-layer) package lemon cake mix with
    pudding
1/4 cup milk
2 eggs

8 ounces cream cheese, softened
1/4 cup sugar
1 tablespoon lemon juice
1 teaspoon grated lemon zest
1/2 cup chopped nuts

DIRECTIONS:

Preheat the oven to 350 degrees.

Cut the butter into the cake mix in a large mixing bowl until the mixture is crumbly. Reserve 1 cup for the topping. Add the milk and eggs to the remaining crumb mixture. Beat for 2 minutes. Pour into a greased 9×13-inch cake pan.

Beat the cream cheese, sugar, lemon juice and lemon zest in a mixing bowl until smooth. Drop by teaspoonfuls onto the batter.

Mix the nuts and reserved crumb mixture in a bowl. Sprinkle over the top. Bake for 35 to 40 minutes or until the cake tests done.

PHOTOGRAPH LEFT: CREOLE GUMBO

HARVEST FEAST

Friends and family will certainly enjoy every morsel in this exceptional menu. You may serve it at Thanksgiving for a delicious variation of the traditional meal or use it to treat friends to a truly special dinner.

Hot Feta Artichoke Dip

MAKES 2 CUPS

1 (14-ounce) can artichoke hearts, drained and chopped
8 ounces crumbled feta cheese
1 cup mayonnaise

1/2 cup shredded Parmesan cheese
1 (2-ounce) jar diced pimento, drained
1 garlic clove, minced

DIRECTIONS:

Preheat the oven to 350 degrees.

Combine the artichoke hearts, feta cheese, mayonnaise, Parmesan cheese, pimento and garlic in a bowl and mix well. Spoon into a 9-inch pie plate or 3-cup shallow baking dish.

Bake for 20 to 25 minutes or until light brown. Serve with crackers.

Note: You may prepare ahead and refrigerate for 8 to 12 hours. Bake for 30 to 35 minutes.

Bacon-Wrapped Fruit

SERVES VARIABLE

dried fruit, such as dates, apricots, apples or pears

slices of bacon, cut into 3-inch lengths

DIRECTIONS:

Preheat the broiler.

Wrap each piece of dried fruit with the bacon. Spear each with a wooden pick. Arrange on a rack in a broiler pan.

Broil for 2 to 3 minutes or until the bacon is crisp.

Party Mushroom Appetizers

SERVES 24

1/2 cup flour
1/2 teaspoon paprika
1 cup soft bread crumbs
1/2 cup grated Parmesan cheese
2 teaspoons basil
2 eggs, lightly beaten

2 tablespoons milk
1 pound fresh white mushrooms
1/4 cup (1/2 stick) butter, melted
1/4 cup mayonnaise
1 tablespoon Dijon mustard
1 tablespoon snipped fresh parsley

DIRECTIONS:

Preheat the oven to 450 degrees.

Mix the flour and paprika in a sealable plastic bag. Mix the bread crumbs, cheese and basil in a sealable plastic bag. Beat the eggs and milk in a bowl.

Clean the mushrooms and remove the stems. Shake the mushrooms in the flour mixture. Dip in the egg mixture. Shake in the bread crumb mixture, pressing to coat.

Arrange the mushrooms cap side down in a lightly greased or parchment paper-lined 10×15-inch baking pan. Drizzle with the butter.

Bake for 10 minutes or until golden brown.

Combine the mayonnaise, Dijon mustard and parsley in a small bowl and mix well. Serve with the mushrooms for dipping.

THE BEST LITTLE
JALAPEÑO CORN BREAD
IN TEXAS

CROWN ROAST OF
PORK WITH
CRANBERRY SAUSAGE
STUFFING

HARVEST FEAST
APPLE CAKE

PEAR CAKE WITH
PINE NUTS

APPLE CRANBERRY
COBBLER

PERFECT
WHIPPED CREAM

PECAN PUMPKIN PIE

KIOKI COFFEE

Pumpkin Salad

SERVES 12

To chill extra beverages for a party, fill the basket of your washing machine with ice cubes and then nestle the cans and bottles in the ice. When the party is over and the ice is melted, simply run the washer's spin cycle to drain the water.

2 small pumpkins, rinsed
4 garlic cloves, peeled
salt to taste
2 tablespoons butter, melted
lemon juice to taste
1 cup long grain white rice, cooked
2 cups peas, cooked
2 1/4 cups shredded white cabbage, blanched
1 red bell pepper, seeded and chopped
1 fennel bulb, chopped

1 Jerusalem artichoke, scraped and shredded
4 tomatoes, peeled and chopped
1/3 cup golden raisins
1 small apple, shredded
1 tablespoon chopped fresh parsley
1 teaspoon caraway seeds
2 tablespoons wine vinegar
1 tablespoon olive oil
coarsely ground pepper to taste

DIRECTIONS:

Preheat the oven to 350 degrees.

Cut off the tops of the pumpkins about 1/4 of the way down and reserve. Scoop out the seeds and pulp from the pumpkins. Rub the insides of the pumpkins with a cut garlic clove and sprinkle with salt. Place 1 garlic clove in each pumpkin. Replace the tops. Arrange on baking sheets.

Bake for 35 minutes. Brush the inside of the pumpkins with the butter and sprinkle with salt. Bake for 15 minutes.

Scoop out about 1/2 of the pulp from each pumpkin into a bowl. Mash 3 tablespoons of the pumpkin with the cooked garlic in a bowl. Crush the remaining garlic cloves. Add the mashed pumpkin and the remaining garlic to the pumpkin pulp and mix well. Sprinkle with lemon juice. Spread inside the pumpkins. Let stand until cool.

Combine the rice, peas, cabbage, bell pepper, fennel, artichoke, tomatoes, raisins, apple, parsley, caraway seeds, wine vinegar, olive oil and pepper in a large bowl and mix well. Spoon into the pumpkins and serve.

Garlic Mashed Potatoes

SERVES 4

12 garlic cloves
1 teaspoon olive oil
2 pounds new potatoes
2 tablespoons butter, melted

2 tablespoons half-and-half
1/2 teaspoon salt
pinch of pepper

DIRECTIONS:

Preheat the oven to 350 degrees.

Toss the garlic in the olive oil in a small baking dish to coat. Cover with foil.

Bake for 30 minutes. Remove from the oven to cool.

Remove the skins from the garlic. Mash the garlic with a fork in a bowl to form a paste.

Fill a large stockpot 1/2 full of water. Bring to a boil. Add the potatoes. Cook for 30 minutes; drain.

Combine the potatoes, butter and garlic in a large bowl. Add the half-and-half, salt and pepper. Mash with a potato masher until smooth.

Green Beans with Toasted Walnuts and Tarragon

SERVES 4 TO 6

21/2 quarts water (10 cups)
1 pound green beans, trimmed
1 teaspoon salt
1/4 cup coarsely chopped walnuts, toasted

11/2 tablespoons minced fresh tarragon
11/2 tablespoons walnut oil
salt and pepper to taste

DIRECTIONS:

Bring the water to a boil in a large saucepan. Add the green beans and 1 teaspoon salt. Cook for 5 minutes or until tender; drain.

Combine the green beans, walnuts and tarragon in a large bowl and mix well. Drizzle with the walnut oil and toss gently to evenly coat. Season with salt and pepper to taste. Serve immediately.

Note: You may substitute basil or parsley for the tarragon.

Sweet Potato Soufflé

SERVES 4 TO 6

2 cups mashed cooked fresh or canned
   sweet potatoes
1/4 cup (1/2 stick) butter, melted
1/2 cup evaporated milk
2 eggs
1/2 cup sugar
1/2 teaspoon cinnamon

1/2 teaspoon nutmeg
1 teaspoon vanilla extract
3/4 cup crisp rice cereal
1/2 cup chopped pecans
1/2 cup packed light brown sugar
1/2 cup (1 stick) butter, softened

DIRECTIONS:

Preheat the oven to 350 degrees.

Process the sweet potatoes, 1/4 cup butter, evaporated milk, eggs, sugar, cinnamon, nutmeg and vanilla in a blender until smooth. Pour into a greased 1 1/2-quart baking dish.

Combine the cereal, pecans, brown sugar and butter in a bowl and mix well with a fork. Sprinkle over the sweet potato mixture.

Bake for 25 minutes.

Julienne of Carrots and Parsnips

SERVES 8

4 or 5 young medium parsnips
4 or 5 medium carrots
1/2 cup (1 stick) unsalted butter

2 teaspoons light brown sugar
salt and freshly ground pepper to taste
minced fresh parsley to taste

DIRECTIONS:

Cut the parsnips and carrots into julienne strips. Melt the butter in a saucepan. Add the parsnips and carrots. Add enough water to almost cover. Sprinkle with the brown sugar, salt and pepper.

Simmer, partially covered, for 20 minutes or until tender. Boil rapidly to evaporate the liquid if necessary. Sprinkle with parsley.

Bleu Cheese Popovers

Freshly ground pepper always tastes better than preground pepper.

2 eggs
1 cup milk
2 tablespoons unsalted butter, melted
1 cup flour

1/2 teaspoon kosher salt
1/8 teaspoon freshly ground pepper
1 1/4 ounces crumbled bleu cheese
1 tablespoon coarsely chopped fresh thyme

DIRECTIONS:

Whisk the eggs, milk, butter, flour, kosher salt and pepper in a large bowl until smooth. Whisk in the cheese and thyme. Pour into an airtight container. Chill, covered, for 2 hours or up to 1 day.

Preheat the oven to 425 degrees.

Butter forty-eight 1 1/2-inch muffin cups generously. Fill each cup with the chilled batter.

Bake for 15 to 18 minutes or until puffed and golden brown. Serve warm.

The Best Little Jalapeño Corn Bread in Texas

SERVES 8

1 package corn bread mix
1 egg
1/2 cup chopped green onions
1 (8-ounce) can cream-style corn

1/4 cup chopped jalapeño chiles
3/4 cup shredded Cheddar cheese
1 tablespoon sugar
2 tablespoons vegetable oil

DIRECTIONS:

Preheat the oven to 425 degrees.

Combine the corn bread mix, egg, green onions, corn, jalapeño chiles, cheese, sugar and oil in a bowl and mix well. Pour into a greased cast-iron skillet or 9-inch pie plate.

Bake for 25 minutes or until golden brown.

Note: Omit the sugar if using Jiffy brand corn bread mix.

Crown Roast of Pork with Cranberry Sausage Stuffing

1 (16-rib) crown roast of pork (about 10 pounds)
1/8 teaspoon salt
1/2 teaspoon pepper
8 ounces bulk pork sausage
1 (16-ounce) can whole cranberry sauce

1 (8-ounce) package herb-seasoned stuffing mix
1 1/2 cups chopped cooking apples
1/4 cup (1/2 stick) butter or margarine, melted

DIRECTIONS:

Preheat the oven to 325 degrees.

Season the pork with the salt and pepper. Arrange the pork bone side up on a rack in a shallow roasting pan. Insert a meat thermometer into the pork, making sure not to touch fat or bone.

Brown the sausage in a skillet, stirring until crumbly; drain. Combine the sausage, cranberry sauce, stuffing mix, apples and butter in a bowl and mix well. Spoon into the center of the pork. Cover the stuffing and ends of the ribs with foil.

Bake for 4 hours or until the meat thermometer registers 160 degrees.

Harvest Feast Apple Cake

⟨ᘓ⟩

SERVES 15

Never frost a cake until it is thoroughly cool.

4 cups chopped peeled fresh apples	*2 eggs*
2 cups sugar	*1 cup chopped nuts*
2 cups flour	*2 teaspoons cinnamon*
1 1/2 teaspoons baking soda	*2 teaspoons vanilla extract*
1 teaspoon salt	*Cream Cheese Frosting (below)*
1 cup vegetable oil	

DIRECTIONS:

Combine the apples and sugar in a large bowl and toss to mix. Let stand for 1 hour.

Preheat the oven to 350 degrees.

Add the flour, baking soda, salt, oil, eggs, nuts, cinnamon and vanilla to the apple mixture and mix well by hand. Spoon into a nonstick 9×13-inch cake pan.

Bake for 45 minutes. Remove the pan to a wire rack to cool completely. Spread with Cream Cheese Frosting.

Cream Cheese Frosting

8 ounces cream cheese, softened	*1/2 (16-ounce) package confectioners'*
1/2 cup (1 stick) margarine, softened	*sugar*
	1 teaspoon vanilla extract

DIRECTIONS:

Beat the cream cheese and margarine in a mixing bowl until light and fluffy. Add the confectioners' sugar and vanilla and beat until smooth.

Pear Cake with Pine Nuts

❧

For a festive punch bowl, slice green apples from stem to core. Use a star, diamond, or other decorative cookie cutter to remove cores. Dip the apple slices in lemon juice and float in the punch.

1¼ cups flour
¾ cup sugar
⅛ teaspoon salt
¼ cup (½ stick) butter, chilled and cut into pieces
¼ teaspoon cinnamon
2 tablespoons pine nuts, toasted
⅓ cup fat-free sour cream

¼ cup reduced-fat milk
1 teaspoon grated lemon zest
1 teaspoon vanilla extract
½ teaspoon baking powder
¼ teaspoon baking soda
1 egg
2 cups thinly sliced pears

DIRECTIONS:

Preheat the oven to 350 degrees.

Whisk the flour, sugar and salt in a large bowl. Cut in the butter with a pastry blender until the mixture resembles coarse cornmeal.

Mix ⅓ cup of the flour mixture, cinnamon and pine nuts in a bowl.

Combine the remaining flour mixture, sour cream, milk, lemon zest, vanilla, baking powder, baking soda and egg in a large mixing bowl. Beat at medium speed until blended. Pour into a 9-inch cake pan coated with nonstick cooking spray. Arrange the pear slices evenly over the batter. Sprinkle with the pine nut mixture.

Bake for 45 minutes or until a wooden pick inserted in the center comes out clean. Remove the pan to a wire rack to cool completely.

Apple Cranberry Cobbler

SERVES 6 TO 8

3 cups unpeeled McIntosh apples, cut into cubes

2 cups fresh or frozen cranberries

3/4 cup (or more) sugar

1/2 cup (1 stick) butter or margarine

1 cup rolled oats

1 1/3 cups flour

1/2 cup packed brown sugar

1/2 cup chopped pecans

DIRECTIONS:

Preheat the oven to 350 degrees.

Mix the apples and cranberries in a 1 1/2-quart baking dish. Sprinkle with the sugar.

Melt the butter in a saucepan. Mix the oats and flour in a bowl. Add the melted butter and brown sugar and mix well. Spread over the apple mixture to cover completely, but do not smooth or pack.

Bake for 45 minutes. Sprinkle with the pecans. Bake for 15 minutes longer.

Perfect Whipped Cream

MAKES 4 CUPS

2 cups whipping cream, chilled

2 tablespoons sugar

2 teaspoons vanilla extract

DIRECTIONS:

Chill a nonreactive 2-quart mixing bowl and beaters for a handheld mixer in the freezer for at least 20 minutes.

Add the whipping cream, sugar and vanilla to the chilled bowl. Beat at low speed for 30 seconds or until small bubbles form. Beat at medium speed for 30 seconds or until the beaters leave a trail in the thickening cream. Beat at high speed for 30 seconds or until soft peaks form and the cream is thick and nearly doubled in volume. Beat 10 seconds longer for stiff peaks.

Pecan Pumpkin Pie

SERVES 6 TO 8

1 egg, lightly beaten
1 cup solid-pack pumpkin
1/3 cup sugar or packed brown sugar
1 teaspoon pumpkin pie spice
1 unbaked (9-inch) pie shell
2 eggs, beaten

2/3 cup corn syrup
1/2 cup sugar
3 tablespoons butter, melted
1/2 teaspoon vanilla extract
1 cup pecan halves

DIRECTIONS:

Preheat the oven to 350 degrees.

Combine 1 egg, pumpkin, 1/3 cup sugar and pumpkin pie spice in a bowl and stir to mix well. Spread over the bottom of the pie shell.

Combine 2 eggs, corn syrup, 1/2 cup sugar, butter and vanilla in a bowl and mix well. Stir in the pecans. Spoon over the pumpkin mixture.

Bake for 50 minutes or until the filling is set.

Kioki Coffee

SERVES 1

2 tablespoons Kahlúa
1 tablespoon brandy

1 cup brewed coffee
1 cup whipping cream, whipped

DIRECTIONS:

Pour the Kahlúa and brandy into a mug. Stir in the coffee. Top with the whipped cream.

Winter

❧❧

THE PLEASURES OF THE TABLE ARE OF ALL TIMES AND
IN ALL AGES, OF EVERY COUNTRY AND
OF EVERY DAY; THEY GO HAND IN HAND WITH
ALL OUR OTHER PLEASURES, OUTLAST THEM,
AND IN THE END CONSOLE US FOR THEIR LOSS.

—Brillat-Savarin in *The Physiology of Taste*

Winter is when we share special moments with the people who matter to us the most. Smell the aromas of the season: mulling spices, baked goodies, roasted chestnuts. Carry on your old traditions, while creating some new. Make memories that will stay in your heart for a lifetime.

Feel the warmth of our winter menus. Taste homemade holiday goodies at the Sweets Swap. Sing carols in front of a cozy fire at the Tree Trimming Buffet. Reveal your New Year's resolutions at the Resolutions Dinner Party. Cheer your team to victory during the Super Bowl Party. Share the season with those closest to your heart.

SWEETS SWAP

These wonderful homemade goodies will just melt in your mouth. Your guests will ask you for the "secret recipes" from this scrumptious menu—but it's up to you whether or not you keep the secret!

Cinnamon Praline Drops

MAKES 4 DOZEN

1/2 cup (1 stick) butter, softened
1/2 cup sugar
1/2 cup packed brown sugar
1 egg

11/2 cups flour
11/2 teaspoons vanilla extract
11/2 cups chopped pecans
3/4 cup cinnamon chips

DIRECTIONS:

Preheat the oven to 375 degrees.

Combine the butter, sugar, brown sugar, egg, flour and vanilla in a mixing bowl and mix well. Stir in the pecans and cinnamon chips. Drop by rounded teaspoonfuls onto greased cookie sheets.

Bake for 8 to 10 minutes or until golden brown. Cool on wire racks.

Crescent Cookies

MAKES ABOUT 2 DOZEN

1 cup almonds or pecans, chopped
1 cup (2 sticks) butter or margarine,
    softened

3/4 cup sugar
21/2 cups flour
1 cup sifted confectioners' sugar

DIRECTIONS:

Preheat the oven to 350 degrees.

Combine the almonds, butter, sugar and flour in a large bowl and mix to form a smooth dough. Shape 1 teaspoonful at a time into 11/2-inch crescents. Arrange on ungreased cookie sheets.

Bake for 15 minutes or until light brown. Remove from the oven. Cool for 1 minute. Roll immediately in the confectioners' sugar.

Orange Pecan Balls

MAKES 3 DOZEN

1 (12-ounce) package vanilla wafers
1 (1-pound) package confectioners' sugar
1/2 cup (1 stick) butter, melted

1 (6-ounce) can frozen orange juice
   concentrate, thawed
1 cup chopped pecans

DIRECTIONS:

Crush the vanilla wafers in a sealable plastic bag. Reserve enough confectioners' sugar for coating. Combine the vanilla wafers, remaining confectioners' sugar, butter and orange juice concentrate in a large bowl and mix well. Stir in the pecans. Shape into small balls. Roll in the reserved confectioners' sugar. Arrange on a tray. Chill, covered, for 8 to 12 hours or until firm.

Chocolate Lemon Cream Candies

MAKES 6 DOZEN

16 ounces cream cheese, softened
2 tablespoons grated lemon zest
3 tablespoons fresh lemon juice

1 teaspoon lemon extract
1 cup sifted confectioners' sugar
24 ounces chocolate candy coating

DIRECTIONS:

Beat the cream cheese, lemon zest, lemon juice, lemon extract and confectioners' sugar in a mixing bowl at medium speed until smooth. Freeze, covered, for 2 hours.

Shape the cream cheese mixture into 1-inch balls. Arrange on a baking sheet lined with waxed paper. Freeze, covered, for 1 hour. Let stand at room temperature for 10 minutes.

Microwave the chocolate candy coating in a 1-quart microwave-safe bowl on High for 1 1/2 minutes or until melted, stirring twice. Dip the balls into the chocolate mixture and arrange on waxed paper. Let stand until firm.

Oatmeal Cheesecake Cranberry Bars

MAKES 3 DOZEN

2 cups flour
1 1/4 cups quick-cooking oats
3/4 cup packed brown sugar
1 cup (2 sticks) butter or margarine
11 ounces cream cheese, softened
1/2 cup sugar

2 eggs
2 teaspoons lemon juice
1 teaspoon vanilla extract
1 (16-ounce) can whole cranberry sauce
2 teaspoons cornstarch

DIRECTIONS:

Preheat the oven to 350 degrees.

Mix the flour, oats and brown sugar in a large bowl. Cut in the butter with a pastry blender until the mixture resembles coarse crumbs. Reserve 1 1/2 cups of the crumb mixture. Press the remaining crumb mixture into a greased 9×13-inch baking pan.

Bake for 15 minutes.

Beat the cream cheese and sugar at medium speed in a mixing bowl until light and fluffy. Beat in the eggs, lemon juice and vanilla. Spread over the baked layer.

Mix the cranberry sauce and cornstarch in a small bowl. Spread carefully over the cream cheese layer. Sprinkle with the reserved crumb mixture.

Bake for 40 minutes or until set. Cool on a wire rack. Chill, covered, for 3 hours or longer. Cut into bars.

Chocolate Pecan Pie Squares

1 cup flour
1/2 cup sugar
1/2 teaspoon baking soda
1/4 teaspoon salt
1/4 cup (1/2 stick) margarine
2 cups (12 ounces) semisweet chocolate
   chips or milk chocolate chips

1 cup corn syrup
3 eggs
1/3 cup sugar
1/4 cup (1/2 stick) margarine
1/2 teaspoon salt
1 cup chopped pecans

DIRECTIONS:

Preheat the oven to 350 degrees.

Mix the flour, 1/2 cup sugar, baking soda and 1/4 teaspoon salt in a small bowl. Cut in 1/4 cup margarine until crumbly. Press evenly into a 9×13-inch baking pan. Bake for 7 minutes.

Melt the chocolate chips in a saucepan, stirring constantly. Combine the corn syrup, eggs, 1/3 cup sugar, 1/4 cup margarine and 1/2 teaspoon salt in a mixing bowl and beat well. Add the melted chocolate and mix well. Stir in the pecans. Pour over the baked layer.

Bake for 35 to 40 minutes or until set. Cool on a wire rack. Cut into squares. Serve with whipped cream or vanilla ice cream.

Caramel Candy

MAKES ABOUT 4 POUNDS

4 cups sugar
1 1/2 cups (3 sticks) butter
2 cups miniature marshmallows
1 cup buttermilk

1 tablespoon white corn syrup
1 teaspoon baking soda
2 cups chopped pecans

DIRECTIONS:

Combine the sugar, butter, marshmallows, buttermilk, corn syrup and baking soda in a large saucepan.

Bring to a boil, stirring constantly. Stir in the pecans. Cook to 240 to 248 degrees on a candy thermometer, firm-ball stage, stirring constantly. Remove from the heat. Cool for 10 minutes. Beat with a spoon until thickened. Pour onto buttered waxed paper to cool. Cut into pieces.

Cherry Surprise Balls

A bouquet of pinecones and ribbon makes a festive holiday centerpiece.

MAKES 4 TO 5 DOZEN

1 cup (2 sticks) butter, softened
1/2 cup sifted confectioners' sugar
2 cups sifted cake flour
1 teaspoon vanilla extract

1/2 cup chopped pecans
1 pound whole candied red cherries
sifted confectioners' sugar for rolling

DIRECTIONS:

Cream the butter and 1/2 cup confectioners' sugar in a mixing bowl until light and fluffy. Add the cake flour and vanilla and mix well. Stir in the pecans. Shape the dough into a ball and wrap in waxed paper. Chill for 2 hours.

Shape enough dough around each cherry to make a 3/4-inch ball. Arrange on ungreased cookie sheets. Chill for 15 minutes.

Preheat the oven to 350 degrees.

Bake for 20 minutes. Remove from the oven. Cool slightly. Roll the warm cookies in sifted confectioners' sugar.

Viennese Pastry Envelopes

MAKES ABOUT 3 1/2 DOZEN

3/4 cup (1 1/2 sticks) unsalted butter,
    softened
6 ounces cream cheese, softened
2 egg yolks, or 3 small egg yolks

1 1/3 cups flour
whole strawberry jam
confectioners' sugar

DIRECTIONS:

Preheat the oven to 325 degrees.

Beat the butter, cream cheese and egg yolks in a medium bowl until smooth. Stir in the flour to form a soft dough.

Roll into a rectangle 1/4 inch thick on a floured surface. Cut into 2-inch squares. Place 1/2 teaspoon jam in the center of each square. Fold the 4 corners toward the center and press the edges firmly together. Arrange on an ungreased baking sheet.

Bake for 15 minutes or until golden brown, watching closely to prevent overbrowning.

Remove from the oven. Sprinkle with confectioners' sugar.

Chocolate Squares

1 cup (2 sticks) unsalted butter or
   margarine, slightly softened
1/2 cup packed light brown sugar
1/2 cup sugar
2 egg yolks
1 cup flour

1 cup quick-cooking oats
14 ounces milk chocolate
1 cup (2 sticks) plus 2 tablespoons
   unsalted butter or margarine
3/4 cup finely chopped walnuts

DIRECTIONS:

Preheat the oven to 350 degrees.

Cream 1 cup butter, brown sugar and sugar in a mixing bowl until light and fluffy. Beat in the egg yolks. Stir in the flour and oats. Press into a lightly greased 11×17-inch shallow baking pan.

Bake for 20 minutes or until set.

Melt the chocolate and 1 cup plus 2 tablespoons butter in a saucepan, stirring constantly. Spread over the baked layer. Sprinkle with the walnuts. Cut into squares.

Almond Butter Bars

3/4 cup (1½ sticks) butter
1½ cups sugar
2 eggs
1/2 teaspoon salt
1½ teaspoons almond extract

1 teaspoon vanilla extract
1½ cups flour
1 tablespoon sugar
3/4 cup slivered almonds (optional)

DIRECTIONS:

Preheat the oven to 350 degrees.

Melt the butter in a saucepan. Combine the butter and 1½ cups sugar in a large bowl and stir until smooth. Add the eggs and beat until the batter is creamy and pale yellow. Add the salt, flavorings and flour and stir briskly until the batter is smooth. Spread evenly in a greased 8×8-inch baking pan. Sprinkle with 1 tablespoon sugar. Top with the slivered almonds.

Bake on the middle oven rack for 35 to 45 minutes or until light brown on top and a wooden pick inserted in the center comes out with a few sticky crumbs. Cool for at least 30 minutes before cutting into bars.

Crème de Menthe Squares

1/2 cup (1 stick) butter
1/2 cup baking cocoa
1/2 cup confectioners' sugar
1 egg, beaten
1 teaspoon vanilla extract
2 cups graham cracker crumbs

1/2 cup (1 stick) butter
1/3 cup green crème de menthe
3 cups confectioners' sugar
1/4 cup (1/2 stick) butter
1 1/2 cups (9 ounces) semisweet chocolate
chips

DIRECTIONS:

Melt 1/2 cup butter and the baking cocoa in a saucepan, stirring constantly. Remove from the heat. Add 1/2 cup confectioners' sugar, egg and vanilla and mix well. Stir in the graham cracker crumbs. Press into an ungreased 9×13-inch dish. Chill in the refrigerator.

Melt 1/2 cup butter in a saucepan. Combine the melted butter and crème de menthe in a mixing bowl and mix well. Beat in 3 cups confectioners' sugar gradually at low speed until smooth. Spread over the graham cracker mixture. Chill for 1 hour.

Melt 1/4 cup butter and chocolate chips in a saucepan over low heat until smooth, stirring constantly. Spread over the crème de menthe mixture. Chill for 2 hours or longer.

Cut into small squares by making 8 cuts horizontally and 12 cuts vertically. Store in the refrigerator.

Note: You may also freeze until ready to serve. To avoid raw eggs that may carry salmonella, we suggest using an equivalent amount of pasteurized egg substitute.

Banana Pound Cake

SERVES 16

To keep punch cold without diluting its flavor, freeze some of the punch in a ring mold before the party. During the party, simply float the frozen ring in the punch bowl.

3 cups flour
1/2 teaspoon baking powder
1/2 teaspoon baking soda
1/2 teaspoon salt
1 cup (2 sticks) butter or margarine, softened
1/2 cup shortening
2 cups packed light brown sugar

1 cup sugar
5 eggs
1/2 cup milk
1 banana, mashed
1 cup chopped pecans
2 teaspoons vanilla extract
Caramel Glaze (below)

DIRECTIONS:

Preheat the oven to 325 degrees.

Mix the flour, baking powder, baking soda and salt together.

Beat the butter and shortening in a large mixing bowl at medium speed until creamy. Add the brown sugar and sugar gradually, beating constantly for 5 to 7 minutes. Add the eggs 1 at a time, beating until the yellow disappears. Add the flour mixture alternately with the milk, beating at low speed until blended after each addition and beginning and ending with the flour mixture. Stir in the banana, pecans and vanilla. Pour into a greased and floured 10-inch tube pan.

Bake for 65 minutes or until a wooden pick inserted in the center comes out clean. Cool in the pan on a wire rack for 10 minutes. Remove from the pan and cool completely on a wire rack. Drizzle with Caramel Glaze.

Caramel Glaze

1/4 cup (1/2 stick) butter or margarine, softened
1/4 cup packed light brown sugar

1/4 cup sugar
1/4 cup whipping cream
1 teaspoon vanilla extract

DIRECTIONS:

Bring the butter, brown sugar, sugar and cream to a boil in a heavy saucepan over high heat, stirring frequently. Boil for 1 minute; do not stir. Remove from the heat. Stir in the vanilla. Cool until slightly thickened.

Chocolate Rum Cake

1/2 cup chopped pecans

1 (2-layer) package devil's food cake mix

1 (4-ounce) package vanilla instant
   pudding mix

1/2 cup light rum

1/2 cup water

1/2 cup vegetable oil

4 eggs

1/2 cup (1 stick) butter

1/2 cup sugar

1/4 cup rum

1/4 cup water

confectioners' sugar

DIRECTIONS:

Preheat the oven to 325 degrees.

   Grease a bundt pan. Sprinkle the pecans in the bottom of the prepared pan.

   Beat the cake mix, pudding mix, 1/2 cup rum, 1/2 cup water, oil and eggs in a large mixing bowl at medium speed for 3 minutes. Spoon into the prepared pan.

   Bake for 1 hour or until the top springs back when lightly touched.

   Bring the butter, sugar, 1/4 cup rum and 1/4 cup water to a boil in a saucepan. Boil for 2 minutes, stirring constantly.

   Spoon the glaze over the top of the hot cake in the pan. Cool for 30 minutes. Invert onto a cake plate. Sprinkle with confectioners' sugar.

French Chocolate

SERVES 8

3 ounces bitter chocolate
1/2 cup cold water
2/3 cup sugar

pinch of salt
1 cup whipping cream, whipped
hot milk

DIRECTIONS:

Combine the chocolate and water in a saucepan. Cook over low heat for
4 minutes, stirring constantly. Remove from the heat. Add the sugar and salt.
Cook for 4 minutes. Remove from the heat. Cool completely. Fold in the
whipped cream.

To serve, place 1 heaping teaspoon chocolate mixture in each serving cup.
Fill each with hot milk.

Maple Coffee

SERVES 2

1 cup half-and-half
1/4 cup maple syrup

1 cup hot brewed coffee
sweetened whipped cream

DIRECTIONS:

Cook the half-and-half and maple syrup in a saucepan over medium heat
until heated through, stirring constantly; do not boil. Stir in the coffee. Serve
with the whipped cream.

For an interesting and aromatic holiday centerpiece, make a spiced orange candle. You will need a votive candle, orange, pen, paring knife, and whole cloves. Using the votive as a template, trace a circle on the top of the orange. Cut the circle and trim to fit the candle exactly. Spoon out the pulp. Set the candle in the orange. Stud the rim of the opening with whole cloves.

Show that special someone just how much he or she means to you with this cozy, romantic dinner.

Fresh Watercress Baby Tomato Salad with Sherry Vinaigrette

SERVES 4 TO 6

1/2 cup olive oil
1/4 cup sherry vinegar
1 tablespoon honey
1/4 cup minced shallots
1 teaspoon Dijon mustard

salt and freshly ground pepper to taste
1/2 pint red currant tomatoes
1/2 pint yellow teardrop tomatoes
1/2 cup julienned Vidalia onion
4 small bunches fresh watercress, torn

DIRECTIONS:

Whisk the olive oil, vinegar, honey, shallots and Dijon mustard in a small bowl to blend. Season with salt and pepper. Add the tomatoes and onion. Marinate, covered, at room temperature for 1 hour.

Place the watercress in a large salad bowl. Add the tomato mixture and toss to mix. Season with salt and pepper.

Note: You may use a medley of baby tomatoes. You may substitute fresh baby spinach for the watercress.

Sautéed Baby Vegetables

12 baby carrots
salt to taste
1/4 cup (1/2 stick) butter
8 ounces baby zucchini, trimmed

8 ounces baby pattypan squash, trimmed
8 ounces baby yellow crookneck or yellow
    zucchini squash, trimmed
pepper to taste

DIRECTIONS:

Cook the carrots in boiling salted water to cover in a large saucepan for
2 minutes; drain. Rinse with cold water; drain.

Melt the butter in a large heavy skillet over medium-high heat. Add the
carrots and remaining vegetables. Sauté for 10 minutes or until the vegetables
are tender-crisp and beginning to brown. Season with salt and pepper. Spoon
into a large bowl to serve.

Spinach Sauté

2 teaspoons olive oil
1 cup sliced mushrooms
1 teaspoon minced garlic

1 pound fresh spinach, trimmed
2 tablespoons grated Parmesan cheese
freshly ground pepper to taste

DIRECTIONS:

Heat the olive oil in a nonstick skillet over medium-high heat. Add the
mushrooms and garlic. Sauté until tender. Add the spinach. Sauté until the
spinach is wilted. Remove from the heat.

Add the cheese. Sprinkle with pepper. Serve immediately.

Beef Fillets with Stilton Portobello Sauce

For beautiful, formal place cards with a natural touch, spray paint large, sturdy leaves, such as magnolia leaves, gold. Once the leaves are dry, write the names of your guests on the leaves with a black permanent marker or paint pen.

SERVES 6

6 (6-ounce) beef tenderloin fillets
2 teaspoons chopped fresh tarragon
1/2 teaspoon freshly ground pepper
5 tablespoons butter or margarine
8 ounces portobello mushroom caps, sliced

1/3 cup dry red wine
1/2 cup sour cream
3 ounces Stilton or bleu cheese, crumbled

Garnish:
sprigs of fresh tarragon

DIRECTIONS:

Rub the fillets with the chopped tarragon and pepper. Melt 2 tablespoons of the butter in a large skillet over medium-high heat. Add the fillets. Cook for 4 to 5 minutes on each side or to the desired degree of doneness. Remove from the skillet and keep warm.

Melt the remaining 3 tablespoons butter in the skillet. Add the mushrooms. Sauté for 3 to 4 minutes or until tender. Add the wine. Cook for 1 to 2 minutes, stirring to deglaze the skillet. Stir in the sour cream. Add 1/4 cup of the cheese. Cook until melted, stirring constantly.

To serve, drizzle the sauce over the fillets. Sprinkle with the remaining cheese. Garnish with sprigs of tarragon.

Note: You may use two 8- or 10-ounce fillets, but adjust the cooking time.

PHOTOGRAPH RIGHT:

BEEF FILLETS WITH STILTON PORTOBELLO SAUCE

Roasted Rosemary Potatoes

3 large potatoes
3 tablespoons olive oil
1¹/2 tablespoons Dijon mustard
1 tablespoon minced fresh rosemary
2 teaspoons lemon zest

2 tablespoons fresh lemon juice
2 teaspoons crushed red pepper flakes
3 tablespoons grated Parmesan cheese
1¹/2 teaspoons kosher salt
¹/4 teaspoon freshly ground black pepper

DIRECTIONS:

Preheat the oven to 425 degrees.

Cut the potatoes into wedges. Rinse and pat dry. Arrange the potatoes in a single layer in a roasting pan.

Combine the olive oil, Dijon mustard, rosemary, lemon zest, lemon juice, red pepper flakes, cheese, kosher salt and black pepper in a medium bowl and blend well. Pour over the potatoes and toss to coat.

Bake for 20 minutes; turn. Bake for 20 minutes longer.

The Most Decadent and Elegant Chocolate Mousse

SERVES 6 TO 8

³/4 cup (1¹/2 sticks) butter, softened
1¹/2 cups sugar
¹/2 teaspoon almond extract
1 tablespoon brandy
3 egg yolks
1 cup (6 ounces) chocolate chips, melted

3 egg whites, stiffly beaten
2 cups whipping cream, stiffly beaten

Garnishes:
whipped cream
dark chocolate curls

DIRECTIONS:

Beat the butter and sugar in a mixing bowl for 5 minutes or until no longer grainy. Add the almond extract, brandy and egg yolks. Beat for 3 to 4 minutes. Stir in the melted chocolate chips. Fold in the stiffly beaten egg whites and whipped cream. Spoon into stemmed glasses. Garnish with whipped cream and dark chocolate curls. Serve with pirouettes.

Note: You may prepare a day ahead and store in the refrigerator. Do not substitute margarine for the butter. To avoid raw eggs that may carry salmonella, we suggest using an equivalent amount of pasteurized egg substitute.

TREE TRIMMING BUFFET

Invite your friends to a tree trimming party, and start the holiday season in festive fashion.

Old Virginia Wassail Punch

SERVES 30

2 quarts sweet apple cider
2 cups orange juice
1 cup lemon juice
4 cups pineapple juice

1 cup sugar
1 cinnamon stick
1 teaspoon whole cloves

DIRECTIONS:

Combine the apple cider, orange juice, lemon juice, pineapple juice and sugar in a stainless steel percolator and stir to mix. Place the cinnamon stick and whole cloves in the percolator basket.

Perk for 18 to 20 minutes. Pour into 4-ounce cups to serve.

Kahlúa Brie

SERVES 12

1 (14-ounce) wheel Brie cheese
1 tablespoon butter
1 cup finely chopped pecans, toasted

1/3 cup Kahlúa
1/4 cup packed brown sugar

DIRECTIONS:

Remove the rind from the top of the cheese. Place the cheese on a microwave-safe platter.

Heat the butter in a saucepan until melted. Stir in the pecans.

Cook for 5 minutes, stirring frequently. Stir in the Kahlúa and brown sugar.

Spoon the pecan mixture over the cheese, spreading to the edge. Microwave on High for 45 seconds or until bubbly.

Serve with melba toast rounds or assorted crackers.

Menu

OLD VIRGINIA WASSAIL PUNCH

KAHLÚA BRIE

CASHEW, CRAB AND ARTICHOKE DIP

BAKED SALAMI

SOUTHERN SALAD

STUFFED SQUASH

RICE PILAF

TANGY GREEN BEANS

POTATO BLEU CHEESE CASSEROLE

DEEP-FRIED TURKEY

PUMPKIN MUFFINS

ALMOND BREAD

PUMPKIN CHOCOLATE CHEESECAKE

HOLIDAY CRANBERRY PIE

OATMEAL TOFFEE COOKIES

Cashew, Crab and Artichoke Dip

SERVES 8 TO 12

1 red bell pepper, chopped
1 green bell pepper, chopped
3 green onions, sliced
2 jalapeño chiles, chopped
   (about 2 tablespoons)
2 teaspoons olive oil

2 (6-ounce) cans lump crab meat, drained
1 (14-ounce) can artichoke hearts,
   drained and chopped
1 cup mayonnaise
1/2 cup grated Parmesan cheese
1 cup cashews

DIRECTIONS:

Preheat the oven to 375 degrees.

Sauté the bell peppers, green onions and jalapeño chiles in the olive oil in a skillet until tender.

Mix the crab meat, artichoke hearts, mayonnaise and cheese in a bowl. Stir into the bell pepper mixture.

Spoon into a greased 1-quart baking dish. Sprinkle with the cashews. Bake for 30 minutes. Serve with crackers.

Baked Salami

SERVES 8 TO 10

1 (10-ounce) jar grape jelly
1 (12-ounce) jar chili sauce
juice of 1 lemon

1/2 cup water
1 large salami, or 3 or 4 small salamis

DIRECTIONS:

Preheat the oven to 225 degrees.

Combine the grape jelly, chili sauce, lemon juice and water in a small bowl and mix well. Score the top of the salami and place in a baking pan. Brush with some of the jelly mixture.

Bake for 3 hours, basting frequently with the remaining jelly mixture. Serve with bread and prepared mustard of choice.

Note: You may substitute other types of jelly for the grape jelly.

Southern Salad

SERVES 6

For a fast way to dress up your salad, score your salad cucumbers with a fork.

6 cups mixed baby greens
1/2 to 1 cup dried cranberries
1 cup pecan halves or chopped pecans

1/2 medium red onion, thinly sliced
crumbled feta cheese to taste
Raspberry Dijon Vinaigrette (below)

DIRECTIONS:

Combine the mixed baby greens, cranberries, pecan halves, red onion and cheese in a large salad bowl and toss to mix.

Add the Raspberry Dijon Vinaigrette and toss to coat.

Raspberry Dijon Vinaigrette

2 tablespoons raspberry vinegar
1/2 teaspoon Dijon mustard
1/2 teaspoon sugar

1/2 teaspoon salt
freshly ground pepper to taste
6 tablespoons olive oil

DIRECTIONS:

Combine the raspberry vinegar, Dijon mustard, sugar, salt and pepper in a bowl and mix until the sugar and salt dissolve.

Whisk in the olive oil.

Stuffed Squash

4 yellow squash
1/2 teaspoon salt
2 tablespoons butter or margarine
2 carrots, shredded
1/2 cup chopped green bell pepper

1 small onion, chopped
1 teaspoon soy sauce
1/4 teaspoon garlic salt
1/4 teaspoon pepper

DIRECTIONS:

Preheat the oven to 325 degrees.

Cook the squash and salt in boiling water to cover in a 2-quart saucepan for 10 minutes; drain and cool.

Cut the squash into halves lengthwise. Scoop out the pulp and reserve, leaving shells 1/4 inch thick.

Melt the butter in a saucepan over medium heat. Add the carrots, bell pepper and onion. Sauté until tender-crisp. Add the soy sauce, garlic salt and pepper. Cook until the vegetables are tender, stirring frequently. Stir in the reserved pulp. Spoon into the squash shells. Arrange the stuffed squash in a 9×13-inch baking pan.

Bake for 10 to 15 minutes or until heated through.

Note: You may sprinkle with a small amount of grated Parmesan cheese and chopped red and green bell peppers.

Rice Pilaf

1/2 cup long grain rice
1/2 cup wild rice
1 small onion, chopped
1 large garlic clove, thinly sliced
1 tablespoon olive oil

1 tablespoon butter
3 cups chicken broth
1/2 cup dried lentils, sorted and rinsed
1/2 to 1 teaspoon curry powder
1 teaspoon salt

DIRECTIONS:

Sauté the long grain rice, wild rice, onion and garlic in the olive oil and butter in a saucepan until the onion is tender and the rice is light golden brown. Add the broth, lentils, curry powder and salt and mix well. Bring to a boil and reduce the heat. Simmer, covered, for 25 minutes.

Tangy Green Beans

SERVES 8

2 tablespoons Dijon mustard
1 tablespoon sugar
1/3 cup butter
salt and pepper to taste

2 tablespoons lemon juice
2 tablespoons vinegar
2 pounds green beans, cooked and drained

DIRECTIONS:

Mix the Dijon mustard, sugar, butter, salt and pepper in a small saucepan.
Bring to a boil and reduce the heat. Simmer until smooth, stirring constantly.
Stir in the lemon juice and vinegar.

Pour over the green beans in a large saucepan. Cook until heated through.

To dot baked foods with butter, freeze a stick of butter, then use a vegetable peeler to shave the desired amount off, letting it fall on the food in fine curls.

Potato Bleu Cheese Casserole

SERVES 6 TO 8

6 medium potatoes
1 1/2 teaspoons salt
1/4 teaspoon white pepper

6 ounces crumbled bleu cheese
4 cups heavy cream

DIRECTIONS:

Preheat the oven to 375 degrees.

Peel the potatoes and cut into thin slices. Toss the potatoes with salt and
white pepper in a bowl. Layer the potatoes and bleu cheese 1/3 at a time in a
buttered 9×13-inch baking dish. Pour the cream over the layers.

Bake, covered, for 45 minutes. Bake, uncovered, for 20 to 25 minutes
longer or until brown.

Deep-Fried Turkey

During the holidays, fill a large, clear glass bowl with Christmas ornaments and ribbons.

1 (10- to 12-pound) turkey
Creole seasoning to taste
1 1/2 cups (3 sticks) butter, melted
1/4 cup onion juice
1/4 cup garlic juice
1/4 cup celery juice

1/4 cup lemon juice
1/4 cup Worcestershire sauce
1/4 cup Tabasco sauce
2 tablespoons liquid smoke
8 gallons peanut oil for deep-frying

DIRECTIONS:

Rub the turkey with Creole seasoning. Wrap in plastic wrap. Chill in the refrigerator for 24 hours.

Combine the butter, onion juice, garlic juice, celery juice, lemon juice, Worcestershire sauce, Tabasco sauce and liquid smoke in a saucepan.

Cook over low heat until heated through, stirring occasionally. Fill a syringe with the warm mixture. Inject into the turkey all over until all of the mixture is used and the turkey is bloated and can no longer hold the liquid.

Chill, covered, for 1 hour.

Preheat the peanut oil in a 60-quart Cajun deep-fat fryer to 350 to 375 degrees. Place the turkey in the fryer basket. Submerge the basket slowly into the hot oil.

Deep-fry for 3 1/2 to 4 minutes per pound or until the turkey is cooked through; drain.

Wrap the turkey in parchment paper. Chill for 20 minutes before slicing.

Pumpkin Muffins

MAKES ABOUT 3 DOZEN

3 cups flour
2 cups sugar
1 teaspoon salt
2 teaspoons baking powder
2 teaspoons baking soda
2 teaspoons pumpkin pie spice

1 teaspoon nutmeg
1/2 teaspoon cinnamon
4 eggs
1 1/2 cups vegetable oil
2 cups cooked pumpkin, or 1 (16-ounce) can pumpkin

DIRECTIONS:

Preheat the oven to 350 degrees.

Mix the flour, sugar, salt, baking powder, baking soda, pumpkin pie spice, nutmeg and cinnamon together.

Beat the eggs, oil and pumpkin in a large bowl until smooth. Add the flour mixture and mix well. Spoon into nonstick muffin cups.

Bake for 30 minutes.

Note: You may bake in miniature muffin cups for 20 to 25 minutes or in 4 loaf pans for 40 minutes.

Almond Bread

MAKES 3 LOAVES

2 cups sugar
4 eggs
1 1/2 cups vegetable oil or corn oil
1 teaspoon vanilla extract or almond extract

3 cups sifted flour
1 1/2 teaspoons baking soda
1 teaspoon salt
1 (12-ounce) can evaporated milk
1 (12-ounce) can almond filling

DIRECTIONS:

Preheat the oven to 350 degrees.

Beat the sugar, eggs, oil and vanilla in a large mixing bowl for 5 minutes. Add the flour, baking soda, salt, evaporated milk and almond filling and beat until smooth. Spoon into 3 greased and floured medium loaf pans.

Bake for 55 minutes or until the loaves test done. Cool in the pans for 10 minutes. Remove to wire racks to cool completely.

Note: You may substitute strawberry or date filling for the almond filling.

Pumpkin Chocolate Cheesecake

Serves 6 to 8

16 ounces cream cheese, softened
2/3 cup sugar
1/2 cup canned pumpkin
1/4 cup heavy cream
1/4 teaspoon cinnamon
1/4 teaspoon ginger

1/8 teaspoon cloves
5 eggs
1 (10-inch) graham cracker pie shell or
    chocolate cookie pie shell
3 ounces semisweet chocolate
1/4 to 1/3 cup heavy cream

DIRECTIONS:

Preheat the oven to 275 degrees.

Beat the cream cheese and sugar in a mixing bowl until smooth. Add the pumpkin, cream, cinnamon, ginger and cloves and mix well. Add the eggs 1 at a time, beating well after each addition. Pour into the pie shell.

Melt the chocolate with the cream in a double boiler, beating constantly. Drizzle over the pumpkin mixture and swirl with a knife to marbleize.

Place the pie plate in a large baking pan. Add enough boiling water to the large baking pan to come halfway up the side of the pie pan.

Bake for 1 hour or until the center is firm. Cool at room temperature for 1 hour. Chill, covered, for 2 hours before serving.

Holiday Cranberry Pie

Serves 6 to 8

2 cups fresh cranberries
1/2 cup sugar
1/2 cup chopped walnuts or pecans
2 eggs

1 cup sugar
1 cup flour
1/2 cup (1 stick) butter, melted
1/4 cup shortening, melted

DIRECTIONS:

Preheat the oven to 325 degrees.

Spread the cranberries in a well-greased 10-inch pie plate. Sprinkle with 1/2 cup sugar and the walnuts.

Beat the eggs in a mixing bowl until foamy. Add 1 cup sugar gradually, beating constantly. Add the flour, butter and shortening and beat well. Pour over the cranberry layer.

Bake for 1 hour. Serve warm or cold with vanilla ice cream.

Note: You may freeze the fresh cranberries to prepare this pie out of season. To prepare as a cobbler, increase this recipe by 1 1/2 times to fill a 9×13-inch baking dish.

Oatmeal Toffee Cookies

To make homemade vanilla extract, pour 1/2 cup vodka into a small container or jar with a tight-fitting lid. Split a 6-inch vanilla bean lengthwise and add it to the vodka. Cover the container tightly and shake once a day for at least 1 week to loosen the seeds from the vanilla pod. Stored in a cool, dark place, the homemade vanilla extract will keep indefinitely.

MAKES ABOUT 2 DOZEN

1¹/2 cups flour
1 teaspoon baking soda
1 cup (2 sticks) unsalted butter, softened
³/4 cup sugar
³/4 cup packed light brown sugar
1 egg

1 teaspoon vanilla extract
1¹/2 cups rolled oats
1 cup dried cherries
1 cup coarsely chopped bittersweet
  chocolate (4¹/2 ounces)
1 cup toffee pieces (5¹/2 ounces)

DIRECTIONS:

Preheat the oven to 350 degrees.

Sift the flour and baking soda together.

Beat the butter, sugar and brown sugar in a mixing bowl at medium-high speed for 2 to 3 minutes or until light and fluffy, scraping down the side of the bowl once or twice. Beat in the egg at high speed. Add the vanilla and beat well. Scrape down the side of the bowl.

Add the flour mixture gradually, beating at low speed until well mixed. Add the oats, dried cherries, chocolate and toffee pieces and beat at low speed until well mixed.

Divide the dough into 3 equal portions. Roll each portion into logs about 1¹/2 inches in diameter using plastic wrap. (You may chill the logs for 1 to 2 days or freeze until ready to use.) Cut the logs into ³/4-inch slices. Arrange on cookie sheets lined with parchment paper.

Bake for 8 to 10 minutes or until golden brown. Remove to wire racks to cool.

RESOLUTIONS DINNER PARTY

As we all know, one of the most common New Year's resolutions is to lose weight. Whether serving this delicious menu before or after you start a diet, we have the perfect chocolate cake for you—one is simply sinful, while the other is surprisingly delicious even though it is low-fat and low-calorie.

Prawn and Pancetta Skewers with Chive Sauce

SERVES 4

20 prawns or large shrimp, peeled and
   deveined
8 slices pancetta or bacon, cut into
   1/2-inch strips
2 shallots, minced
1/4 cup dry white wine

3/4 cup fish stock
1/2 cup cream
3/4 cup (1 1/2 sticks) butter, cut into pieces
salt and pepper to taste
1 tablespoon finely chopped fresh chives
1 tablespoon butter

DIRECTIONS:

Wrap each prawn with a slice of pancetta. Thread 5 wrapped prawns onto each skewer.

Cook the shallots and wine in a small saucepan until of a glaze consistency. Add the stock. Simmer until the mixture is reduced to 2 tablespoons. Add the cream and reduce the heat to low. Whisk in 3/4 cup butter 1 piece at a time until melted. Remove from the heat. Season with salt and pepper. Stir in the chives. Place the saucepan in a hot water bath to keep warm.

Heat 1 tablespoon butter in a medium skillet. Fry the skewers for 2 minutes on each side or until the pancetta is crisp and the prawns turn pink.

To serve, place 1 skewer on each serving plate with 1 tablespoon sauce on the side.

Lucky Black-Eyed Pea Dip

2 (15-ounce) cans black-eyed peas
1 medium onion, chopped
2 garlic cloves, minced

2 jalapeño chiles, minced
1/2 cup (1 stick) margarine
2 (6-ounce) logs garlic cheese

DIRECTIONS:

Drain the black-eyed peas and mash lightly with a fork in a bowl.

Process the black-eyed peas, onion, garlic and jalapeño chiles in a blender until smooth.

Microwave the margarine and garlic cheese in a large microwave-safe dish on Medium for 5 to 6 minutes. Stir until smooth. Add the black-eyed pea mixture and mix well.

Serve hot with corn chips.

Spinach Salad

SERVES 6 TO 8

1 cup pecans
2 tablespoons butter
2 tablespoons brown sugar
2 packages fresh baby spinach
2 pears, cut into bite-size pieces
1 cup crumbled bleu cheese or feta cheese

1 shallot, minced
2 tablespoons sherry wine vinegar
1 tablespoon red wine vinegar
2 teaspoons Dijon mustard
1/3 cup olive oil or vegetable oil
salt and pepper to taste

DIRECTIONS:

Sauté the pecans with the butter and brown sugar in a saucepan for 5 minutes. Cool on paper towels.

Combine the spinach, pears, bleu cheese and sautéed pecans in a large salad bowl and toss to mix.

Whisk the shallot, sherry wine vinegar, red wine vinegar, Dijon mustard, olive oil, salt and pepper in a bowl to blend. Pour over the salad and toss to coat.

Note: You may double the salad dressing if desired.

Garlic Prime Rib Roast

Never cook a cold roast. To bring out the flavor, let it stand at room temperature for at least an hour before cooking.

1 yellow onion, minced
2 or 3 garlic cloves, minced
2 tablespoons pepper
1 tablespoon rosemary

salt to taste
1/4 cup olive oil
1 tablespoon demi-glace or beef base
1 (10-pound or larger) prime rib roast

DIRECTIONS:

Combine the onion, garlic, pepper, rosemary, salt, olive oil and demi-glace in a bowl and mix well. Rub over the prime rib in a shallow pan. Chill, covered, for 8 to 12 hours.

Preheat the oven to 450 degrees.

Arrange the prime rib on a rack in a roasting pan.

Bake on the middle oven rack for 25 minutes. Reduce the oven temperature to 300 degrees. Bake for 3 hours longer or until a meat thermometer inserted into the thickest portion registers 135 degrees.

Remove the prime rib to a cutting board and cover loosely. Let stand for 20 to 30 minutes before carving.

Two-Horseradish Mashed Potatoes

SERVES 8 TO 10

8 large russet potatoes, peeled and
    quartered
cloves of 3 heads of garlic
salt to taste
3 cups heavy cream, reduced by half

1/2 cup (1 stick) butter
1/4 cup prepared horseradish
2 tablespoons wasabi paste
pepper to taste

DIRECTIONS:

Preheat the oven to 250 degrees.

Combine the potatoes, garlic and salt in a large saucepan. Add enough cold water to cover. Bring to a boil. Cook for 30 to 45 minutes or until the potatoes are tender. Do not overcook; drain. Arrange the potatoes on a rack in a roasting pan.

Bake for 15 minutes or until most of the moisture has evaporated.

Beat the potatoes in a mixing bowl at medium speed until smooth. Add 1/2 of the cream, butter, horseradish, wasabi paste, salt and pepper and beat until smooth. Beat in the remaining cream and adjust the seasonings.

Fresh Lemon Carrots

SERVES 4

2 cups julienned or diagonally cut carrots
1/2 teaspoon salt
1/4 cup sugar

2 tablespoons fresh lemon juice
1/4 cup (1/2 stick) butter

DIRECTIONS:

Combine the carrots and salt in a saucepan. Add enough water to cover. Bring to a boil. Boil until the carrots are slightly tender; drain. Plunge immediately into hot water to stop the cooking process; drain.

Bring the sugar, lemon juice and butter to a boil in a saucepan. Boil for 3 minutes, stirring constantly. Stir in the carrots. Serve warm.

The Very Best Chocolate Cake

To help your flower arrangements stay fresh longer, strip the stems so that no leaves touch the water.

SERVES 12

4 ounces bittersweet chocolate
1 1/2 cups (3 sticks) butter
3 cups flour
1 cup baking cocoa
2 teaspoons baking soda
4 eggs
2 1/2 cups sugar
1 cup sour cream

2 teaspoons vanilla extract
2 cups milk
Chocolate Icing (page 179)

Garnishes:
Gold-Brushed Chocolate Leaves (page 179)
organic rose petals or any edible flower

DIRECTIONS:

Preheat the oven to 350 degrees.

Grease three 9-inch cake pans and line with parchment paper.

Melt the bittersweet chocolate and butter in a saucepan, stirring constantly. Remove from the heat to cool slightly.

Whisk the flour, baking cocoa and baking soda together.

Beat the eggs in a mixing bowl for 1 minute. Add the sugar gradually, beating constantly. Add the chocolate mixture and mix well. Add the sour cream and vanilla and mix well. Add the flour mixture alternately with the milk, beating well after each addition and beginning and ending with the flour mixture. Divide evenly among the prepared cake pans.

Bake for 30 minutes or until a wooden pick inserted into the centers comes out clean. Remove to wire racks to cool.

Spread Chocolate Icing between the layers and over the top and side of the cake. Garnish with Gold-Brushed Chocolate Leaves and rose petals.

Note: If the rose petals are purchased from a florist, gently clean the petals and pat dry.

Chocolate Icing

1 cup (2 sticks) butter
1 cup milk
4 cups sugar
16 ounces unsweetened chocolate, chopped

1 cup (2 sticks) butter
1 cup heavy cream
6 egg yolks, beaten

DIRECTIONS:

Combine 1 cup butter, milk and sugar in a heavy saucepan.

Cook to 232 degrees on a candy thermometer, spun-thread stage. Do not stir. Add the chocolate and 1 cup butter. Cook until the butter is partially melted. Stir in the cream and egg yolks. Cook until smooth, stirring constantly.

Remove from the heat and cool to room temperature. Beat the icing until the texture is light.

Gold-Brushed Chocolate Leaves

15 fresh camellia or lemon leaves
8 ounces bittersweet or semisweet
   chocolate, chopped

1 (2-gram) container gold dust

DIRECTIONS:

Wipe the leaves with moist paper towels to clean; pat dry.

Melt the chocolate in a double boiler over simmering water, stirring constantly. Remove from the heat.

Brush the chocolate carefully over the heavily veined side of the camellia leaves with a pastry brush, wiping away any chocolate overflow from the edges. Arrange the leaves on a foil-lined baking sheet.

Freeze for 10 minutes or until firm. Peel the camellia leaves carefully from the chocolate leaves. Return the chocolate leaves to the freezer. Freeze for 10 minutes or longer.

Dip an artist's brush into the gold dust. Brush generously over some of the chocolate leaves. Cover and freeze for up to 3 days.

PHOTOGRAPH ON PAGE 180

Low-Fat and Delicious Chocolate Cake

SERVES 24

2 cups flour
1 cup baking cocoa
2 cups sugar
2 teaspoons baking soda
1 teaspoon baking powder
1/4 teaspoon salt
1/2 teaspoon cinnamon

2 (3-ounce) jars baby food puréed prunes
2 teaspoons vanilla extract
2 eggs, beaten
1 cup skim milk
1 cup strong brewed coffee
Raspberry or Blackberry Sauce (below)

DIRECTIONS:

Preheat the oven to 350 degrees.

Sift the flour, baking cocoa, sugar, baking soda, baking powder, salt and cinnamon into a large bowl.

Mix the prunes, vanilla, eggs, milk and coffee in a bowl until smooth. Add to the flour mixture and stir until blended. Pour into two 9-inch cake pans sprayed with nonstick cooking spray.

Bake for 30 to 35 minutes or until a wooden pick inserted into the centers comes out clean. Cool in the pans for 10 minutes. Invert onto wire racks to cool completely. Serve with Raspberry or Blackberry Sauce.

Note: You may sift confectioners' sugar over the tops of the cakes instead of serving with the sauce. These cakes freeze well.

Raspberry or Blackberry Sauce

1 tablespoon cornstarch
1 tablespoon water
1 tablespoon confectioners' sugar

2 cups fresh or frozen raspberries or
   blackberries

DIRECTIONS:

Dissolve the cornstarch in the water in a small saucepan. Add the confectioners' sugar and raspberries.

Heat until bubbly. Strain through a mesh strainer into a bowl, discarding the solids. Pour into a container.

Chill, covered, until ready to serve.

PHOTOGRAPH LEFT: THE VERY BEST CHOCOLATE CAKE

BREAKFAST IN BED

Choose from a simple, breadbasket meal or a more substantial breakfast with these two delicious menus. Add a bit of fresh seasonal fruit, and you are set either way!

Banana Raspberry Smoothie

SERVES 2 OR 3

2 ripe medium bananas
1 1/2 cups raspberry juice, chilled

1 cup frozen vanilla yogurt, softened
1 cup fresh or frozen raspberries

DIRECTIONS:

Process the bananas, raspberry juice, frozen yogurt and raspberries in a blender until smooth.

Orange Smoothie

SERVES 1 OR 2

1 cup pineapple orange juice, chilled
8 ounces frozen orange yogurt, softened

1/2 cup milk
1 ripe small banana

DIRECTIONS:

Process the pineapple orange juice, orange yogurt, milk and banana in a blender until smooth.

Rich Banana Bread

MAKES 1 LOAF

2 cups flour
1 cup sugar
1/2 teaspoon baking soda
1 teaspoon salt
1/4 cup (1/2 stick) butter, melted
1/4 cup vegetable oil

2 eggs, beaten
1/3 cup sour cream
3 bananas, mashed
1 cup chopped nuts (optional)
1/2 cup (3 ounces) miniature chocolate
    chips (optional)

To make perfectly rounded muffins, grease only the bottom and halfway up the sides of the muffin cups.

DIRECTIONS:

Preheat the oven to 325 degrees.

Sift the flour, sugar, baking soda and salt together.

Mix the butter and oil in a mixing bowl. Add the eggs and sour cream and mix well. Add the flour mixture and beat until smooth. Stir in the bananas, nuts and chocolate chips. Spoon into a nonstick 5×7-inch loaf pan.

Bake for 1 hour. Cool in the pan for 10 minutes. Invert onto a wire rack to cool completely. Store covered for 1 day before slicing.

Apple Carrot Muffins

MAKES 1 DOZEN

1 3/4 cups raisin bran cereal
1 1/4 cups flour
3/4 cup sugar
1 1/4 teaspoons baking soda
1 teaspoon cinnamon
1/4 teaspoon salt

1 egg
3/4 cup buttermilk
1/4 cup canola oil
3/4 cup finely chopped peeled tart apple
3/4 cup grated carrots
1/4 cup chopped nuts

DIRECTIONS:

Preheat the oven to 400 degrees.

Mix the cereal, flour, sugar, baking soda, cinnamon and salt in a large bowl.

Beat the egg, buttermilk and oil in a small mixing bowl. Stir into the cereal mixture just until moistened. Fold in the apple, carrots and nuts. Fill paper-lined muffin cups or cups coated with nonstick cooking spray 3/4 full.

Bake for 20 to 23 minutes or until a wooden pick inserted into the centers comes out clean.

Cranberry Orange Muffins

MAKES 1 DOZEN

With flowers, more is not always
better. One perfect, striking flower
can have more impact than many.

1 cup chopped fresh or frozen cranberries
2 tablespoons sugar
2 cups flour
1/3 cup sugar
2 teaspoons baking powder
1/2 teaspoon salt

1/8 teaspoon grated nutmeg
grated zest of 1 orange
1/2 cup (1 stick) butter
3/4 cup orange juice
1 egg, lightly beaten
sugar for sprinkling

DIRECTIONS:

Preheat the oven to 400 degrees.

Combine the cranberries and 2 tablespoons sugar in a small bowl and toss to mix well.

Sift the flour, 1/3 cup sugar, baking powder, salt, nutmeg and orange zest in a large bowl. Cut in the butter until crumbly. Add the orange juice and egg and stir just until moistened. Fold in the cranberry mixture. Spoon into greased or paper-lined muffin cups.

Bake for 20 to 25 minutes or until the muffins test done. Sprinkle with sugar. Cool in the muffin cups for 5 minutes. Remove to wire racks to cool completely.

Cinnamon Rolls

SERVES 12

1/2 cup (1 stick) butter, melted
1/2 to 3/4 cup packed brown sugar
1 cup chopped pecans

1/2 cup sugar
2 to 3 teaspoons cinnamon
2 (12-count) packages frozen dinner rolls
1 cup (2 sticks) butter, melted

DIRECTIONS:

Mix 1/2 cup butter and brown sugar in a bowl. Pour into a tube pan sprayed lightly with nonstick cooking spray. Sprinkle with the pecans. Mix the sugar and cinnamon in a small bowl. Roll the frozen rolls in 1 cup butter and then in the cinnamon sugar. Arrange in a single layer in the prepared pan. Cover with a dish towel. Place in the oven and close the oven door. Let rise for 8 to 12 hours or until doubled in bulk. Remove from the oven.

Preheat the oven to 350 degrees.

Bake, loosely covered with foil, for 20 to 25 minutes. Bake, uncovered, for 5 minutes longer or until golden brown. Cool in the pan for several minutes. Cover the top of the pan with a serving plate and quickly invert. Let stand for 1 minute to allow all of the brown sugar mixture and pecans to cover the top. Remove the pan.

Stuffed French Toast

4 ounces cream cheese, softened
1/4 cup chopped dates
1/4 cup chopped pecans, toasted
4 teaspoons orange marmalade
2 French bread loaves

4 eggs
1 cup milk
1 teaspoon cinnamon
3 tablespoons butter or margarine
2 tablespoons confectioners' sugar

DIRECTIONS:

Combine the cream cheese, dates, pecans and orange marmalade in a bowl and mix well. Cut the bread into 8 slices 1 inch thick. Cut a horizontal pocket into the top crust of each bread slice. Spoon about 2 teaspoons of the cream cheese mixture into each pocket.

Whisk the eggs, milk and cinnamon in a bowl. Dip the stuffed bread slices into the egg mixture, coating all sides.

Melt the butter in a large nonstick skillet over medium-high heat. Cook the stuffed bread slices in batches for 2 minutes on each side or until golden brown. Sprinkle with the confectioners' sugar.

Gingerbread Pancakes with Maple Whipped Cream

2¹/3 cups water
1/2 cup molasses
4 cups buttermilk pancake mix

1 tablespoon cinnamon
1 tablespoon ginger
Maple Whipped Cream (below)

DIRECTIONS:

Combine the water and molasses in a bowl and blend well.

Mix the pancake mix, cinnamon and ginger in a large bowl. Add the molasses mixture and stir just until moistened.

Heat a lightly oiled griddle or large nonstick skillet over medium heat. Pour 3 tablespoons batter at a time onto the hot griddle. Cook for 4 to 5 minutes or until puffed and light brown, turning once. Cool on wire racks.

Serve with Maple Whipped Cream.

Note: You may freeze in an airtight container with waxed paper separating the layers.

Maple Whipped Cream

1¹/2 cups whipping cream

1/2 cup maple syrup

DIRECTIONS:

Beat the whipping cream and maple syrup in a mixing bowl until soft peaks form. Chill for 2 hours before serving.

SUPER BOWL PARTY

Here is a menu for that famous Sunday we all know and enjoy—the day of the Super Bowl. Cheer your team to victory with this tasty, casual menu.

Black Bean and Cheese Triangles

MAKES 5 DOZEN

1/2 cup olive oil
1/4 teaspoon cumin
1/4 teaspoon cayenne pepper
1 (15-ounce) can black beans, rinsed and drained
salt to taste
1/2 teaspoon sugar

1/2 cup chopped fresh cilantro
1 cup (4 ounces) shredded Monterey Jack cheese
1 plum tomato, finely chopped
1 jalapeño chile, minced
24 sheets phyllo

DIRECTIONS:

Preheat the oven to 375 degrees.

Heat the olive oil, cumin and cayenne pepper in a small saucepan until warm. Combine the black beans, salt, sugar, cilantro, cheese, tomato and jalapeño chile in a medium bowl and stir until the mixture holds together, mashing the beans with the back of the spoon.

Place 1 sheet of phyllo on a work surface. Brush with some of the olive oil mixture. Top with another sheet of phyllo. Brush with some of the remaining olive oil mixture. Cut into 5 equal strips lengthwise. Place 1 teaspoon of the bean mixture at the end of each strip. Fold the corner of the strip diagonally so that the short edge meets the long edge of the strip. Continue folding to form a right-triangle package. Place seam side down on a baking sheet. Brush lightly with the some of the remaining olive oil mixture.

Repeat with the remaining phyllo, filling and olive oil mixture.

Bake for 15 minutes or until brown and crisp.

Menu

BLACK BEAN AND
CHEESE TRIANGLES

CORN DIP

AVOCADO ROLLS

SWEET ONION SLAW

SWEET-AND-SOUR
BAKED BEANS

BEER RIBS

SLOW-COOKER
ENCHILADAS

APPLE BROWNIES

CHOCOLATE CHIP
POUND CAKE

Corn Dip

To freshen dried herbs, add a
pinch of chopped fresh parsley.

❧

SERVES 8 TO 10

2 cups sour cream
3/4 cup mayonnaise
2 (11-ounce) cans Mexicorn, drained
1 (4-ounce) can chopped green chiles

3 green onions, chopped
1/2 to 3/4 cup chopped jalapeño chiles
3 cups (12 ounces) shredded Cheddar
   cheese

DIRECTIONS:

Mix the sour cream and mayonnaise in a large bowl until blended. Add the
Mexicorn, green chiles, green onions, jalapeño chiles and cheese and mix well.
   Chill, covered, for 8 to 12 hours. Serve with corn chip scoops.

Avocado Rolls

❧

SERVES 6 TO 8

1 cup mashed avocado
1 1/2 cups minced cashews
8 ounces cream cheese, softened
1/2 cup (2 ounces) coarsely shredded
   Cheddar cheese
2 teaspoons lime juice

1 garlic clove, crushed
1 1/2 teaspoons salt
1/2 teaspoon Worcestershire sauce
dash of Tabasco sauce
1 ounce paprika

DIRECTIONS:

Combine the avocado, cashews, cream cheese, Cheddar cheese, lime juice,
garlic, salt, Worcestershire sauce and Tabasco sauce in a medium bowl and
mix well. Chill, covered, for 30 minutes.
   Divide the mixture into 2 or 4 equal portions. Shape into cylinders. Roll
in the paprika. Wrap each in foil. Chill for at least 2 hours before serving.
   To serve, cut into slices and serve with cocktail crackers.
   Note: You may freeze the cylinders.

Sweet Onion Slaw

3 sweet onions (about 3¹/2 pounds)
1/4 cup white vinegar
1/4 cup water

1/4 cup sugar
1/4 cup mayonnaise
1/8 teaspoon celery seeds

DIRECTIONS:

Peel the onions and cut into halves. Cut the halves into very thin slices.

Combine the vinegar, water and sugar in a large bowl and stir until the sugar dissolves. Add the onions and toss gently. Chill, tightly covered, for 8 hours, stirring occasionally.

Drain the onions, discarding the marinade. Pat the onions dry and return to the bowl. Stir in the mayonnaise and celery seeds.

Sweet-and-Sour Baked Beans

SERVES 12

3/4 cup packed brown sugar
1 teaspoon dry mustard
1 teaspoon garlic powder
1/2 teaspoon salt
1/2 cup vinegar
3 onions, sliced and coarsely chopped

1 (16-ounce) can lima beans, drained
1 (16-ounce) can kidney beans, drained
2 (16-ounce) cans baked beans
8 slices bacon, cooked and crumbled
4 slices bacon (optional)

DIRECTIONS:

Preheat the oven to 350 degrees.

Combine the brown sugar, dry mustard, garlic powder, salt and vinegar in a bowl and mix well.

Combine the onions and brown sugar mixture in a skillet. Simmer, covered, for 20 minutes. Add the lima beans, kidney beans, baked beans and crumbled bacon and mix well. Spoon into a 3-quart baking dish sprayed with nonstick cooking spray. Arrange the uncooked bacon slices over the top.

Bake for 1 hour.

Beer Ribs

Use freshly ground sea salt instead of preground table salt whenever possible. It greatly enhances the flavor of your food.

2 pounds lean pork spareribs, trimmed and cut into halves crosswise by butcher
salt to taste
1/3 cup dark beer

1/3 cup soy sauce
1/3 cup Dijon mustard
1/4 cup packed dark brown sugar
1 onion, minced
1 teaspoon Worcestershire sauce

DIRECTIONS:

Place the spareribs in a large saucepan and cover with salted water. Bring to a boil and reduce the heat. Simmer for 20 minutes, skimming the froth. Drain and rinse briefly under cold water.

Combine the beer, soy sauce, Dijon mustard, brown sugar, onion and Worcestershire sauce in a large bowl and mix well. Cut the ribs into 1-rib sections. Add to the beer mixture, stirring to coat well. Marinate, covered, at room temperature for 2 hours, stirring occasionally.

Preheat the oven to 350 degrees.

Arrange the ribs meaty side up in single layers in lightly oiled baking pans. Brush with some of the marinade.

Bake on the middle oven rack for 1 hour or until tender and glazed, turning and basting occasionally.

Note: The ribs may be marinated in the refrigerator for 8 to 12 hours. They can also be baked 1 day ahead and refrigerated. Reheat in a baking pan in a preheated 350-degree oven for 10 to 15 minutes or until heated through.

Slow-Cooker Enchiladas

1 pound ground beef
1 cup chopped onion
1/2 cup chopped green bell pepper
1 (16-ounce) can pinto or kidney beans,
    rinsed and drained
1 (16-ounce) can black beans, rinsed and
    drained
1 (10-ounce) can chopped tomatoes with
    green chiles
1/3 cup water

1 teaspoon chili powder
1/2 teaspoon cumin
1/2 teaspoon salt
1/2 teaspoon pepper
1 cup (4 ounces) shredded sharp Cheddar
    cheese
1 cup (4 ounces) shredded Monterey Jack
    cheese
6 (6- or 7-inch) flour tortillas

DIRECTIONS:

Brown the ground beef, onion, and bell pepper in a skillet, stirring until the ground beef is crumbly and the vegetables are tender. Add the pinto beans, black beans, tomatoes with green chiles, water, chili powder, cumin, salt and pepper and mix well. Bring to a boil and reduce the heat. Simmer, covered, for 10 minutes.

Mix the Cheddar cheese and Monterey Jack cheese in a bowl.

Layer 3/4 cup of the ground beef mixture, 1 tortilla and 1/3 cup cheese mixture in a 5-quart slow cooker. Repeat the layers until all of the ingredients are used.

Cook, covered, on Low for 5 to 7 hours or until heated through.

Note: You may also layer in a large baking dish and bake in a preheated 350-degree oven for 1 hour.

Apple Brownies

MAKES 1¹/₃ DOZEN

1/2 cup (1 stick) butter, softened
1 cup sugar
1 cup flour
1 teaspoon cinnamon

1¹/2 tablespoons finely chopped apple
1 egg
1/2 cup nuts

DIRECTIONS:

Preheat the oven to 350 degrees.

Combine the butter, sugar, flour, cinnamon, apple and egg in a bowl and mix well. Stir in the nuts. Spoon into a nonstick 8×8-inch baking pan.

Bake for 30 to 40 minutes or until the brownies rise and the edges pull away from the side of the pan.

Chocolate Chip Pound Cake

SERVES 16

1 (2-layer) package yellow cake mix
1 (4-ounce) package vanilla instant
  pudding mix
1 (4-ounce) package chocolate instant
  pudding mix
4 eggs

1/2 cup vegetable oil
1¹/2 cups water
1 teaspoon vanilla extract
1 cup (6 ounces) semisweet chocolate chips
confectioners' sugar

DIRECTIONS:

Preheat the oven to 325 degrees.

Combine the cake mix, vanilla pudding mix, chocolate pudding mix, eggs, oil, water and vanilla in a large mixing bowl and beat for 2 minutes. Stir in the chocolate chips. Pour into a greased and floured tube or bundt pan.

Bake for 50 to 60 minutes or until the cake tests done. Cool in the pan for 10 minutes. Invert onto a cake plate. Sprinkle the hot cake with confectioners' sugar.

COMFORT FOOD

For a simple, down-home dinner, these recipes are ideal.

Broccoli Salad

SERVES 6 TO 8

2/3 pound bacon
2 heads broccoli
1/2 cup raisins
1 small onion, thinly sliced
6 ounces cream cheese, softened
2 eggs

2 tablespoons grated onion
2 tablespoons vinegar
2 tablespoons sugar
2 tablespoons vegetable oil
1 tablespoon prepared mustard
1/4 teaspoon salt

DIRECTIONS:

Fry the bacon in a skillet until crisp; drain. Crumble the bacon.

Trim the broccoli and cut into florets.

Combine the broccoli, bacon, raisins and sliced onion in a large bowl and toss to mix.

Blend the cream cheese, eggs, 2 tablespoons onion, vinegar, sugar, oil, mustard and salt in a blender until smooth. Pour over the broccoli mixture and toss to coat.

Note: To avoid raw eggs that may carry salmonella, we suggest using an equivalent amount of pasteurized egg substitute.

Beefy Stuffed Pasta Shells

SERVES 8

32 uncooked jumbo pasta shells
1 pound ground beef
1/3 to 1/2 cup minced onion
1/2 teaspoon black pepper
1/4 teaspoon garlic powder
1/4 teaspoon crushed red pepper
1 1/4 cups beef broth
1 (6- or 7-ounce) jar sun-dried tomatoes in oil, drained
1/4 cup pine nuts

3 tablespoons chopped fresh parsley
1/4 cup fresh basil leaves
2 garlic cloves, sliced
1/4 cup olive oil
1/3 cup grated Parmesan cheese
1 (32-ounce) jar spaghetti sauce with tomato and basil
1 1/2 cups (6 ounces) shredded mozzarella cheese
2 tablespoons chopped fresh parsley

DIRECTIONS:

Preheat the oven to 375 degrees.

Cook the pasta shells using the package directions; drain.

Brown the ground beef and onion in a large skillet, stirring until crumbly; drain. Add black pepper, garlic powder and red pepper and mix well. Remove from the heat. Cover and let stand.

Process the beef broth, sun-dried tomatoes, pine nuts, 3 tablespoons parsley, basil and garlic in a blender until blended. Add the olive oil in a slow steady stream and process until combined. Add to the ground beef mixture and mix well. Stir in the Parmesan cheese.

Spoon 1 heaping tablespoonful of the ground beef mixture into each pasta shell. Arrange the stuffed shells in a lightly greased 9×13-inch baking dish. Pour the spaghetti sauce over the top.

Bake, covered, for 20 to 30 minutes or until heated through. Sprinkle with the mozzarella cheese. Bake for 5 minutes or until the cheese melts. Sprinkle with 2 tablespoons parsley.

Mexican Lasagna

SERVES 12

1 1/2 pounds ground turkey or ground beef
1 (17-ounce) can whole kernel corn,
    drained
1 cup picante sauce
1 (15-ounce) can tomato sauce or
    Italian-style tomatoes
1 envelope taco seasoning mix

16 ounces cottage cheese
2 eggs
1 teaspoon oregano
10 corn tortillas
1 1/2 cups (6 ounces) shredded Cheddar
    cheese or Monterey Jack cheese

To improve the flavor of dried herbs, buy whole herbs and roast in a hot, dry saucepan for a couple of minutes and then grind in a coffee grinder.

DIRECTIONS:

Preheat the oven to 375 degrees.

Brown the ground turkey in a skillet, stirring until crumbly; drain. Add the corn, picante sauce, tomato sauce and taco seasoning mix and mix well. Simmer for 5 minutes.

Mix the cottage cheese, eggs and oregano in a bowl.

Arrange 5 of the tortillas overlapping slightly in a lightly greased 9×13-inch baking dish.

Layer 1/2 of the turkey mixture, cottage cheese mixture, remaining tortillas and remaining turkey mixture in the prepared dish. Sprinkle with the Cheddar cheese.

Bake, uncovered, for 30 minutes. Let stand for 10 minutes before serving.

Hot Rolls

SERVES 12

1 cup milk
1 tablespoon yeast
1 tablespoon sugar

3 tablespoons vegetable oil
1 teaspoon salt
3 cups flour

DIRECTIONS:

Microwave the milk in a microwave-safe container for 45 seconds. Add the yeast and stir for 1 minute. Stir in the sugar, oil and salt. Add the flour and mix well.

Knead the dough in a bowl until smooth and elastic. Shape into rolls by rolling a small amount of dough at a time in the palms of your hands until round and smooth. Arrange in a nonstick baking pan.

Let rise, covered, for 1 hour or until doubled in bulk.

Preheat the oven to 400 degrees.

Bake for 20 minutes or until the tops of the rolls are brown. Serve with butter.

Very Vanilla Ice Cream

SERVES 8

6 egg yolks
3/4 cup sugar
1 1/4 cups milk
1 1/4 cups heavy cream

1 1/2 (6-inch) vanilla beans
1/2 teaspoon vanilla extract
pinch of salt

DIRECTIONS:

Beat the egg yolks and sugar in a mixing bowl until light and thick.

Blend the milk and cream in a 2-quart microwave-safe bowl. Cut the vanilla beans into halves lengthwise and scrape the seeds into the bowl. Add the vanilla beans, vanilla and salt.

Microwave, uncovered, on High for 3 minutes. Remove the vanilla beans. Add the milk mixture gradually to the egg yolk mixture, beating constantly at low speed until smooth. Return to the microwave-safe bowl.

Microwave on High for 3 1/2 minutes or until the custard is thick and coats the back of a spoon, whisking and turning the bowl 3 times. Do not overcook. Cool to room temperature. Chill, covered, for 3 hours or longer.

Pour into an ice cream freezer. Freeze using the manufacturer's instructions.

Perfect Apple Crisp

SERVES 6

1/2 cup sugar
2 teaspoons cinnamon
1/4 teaspoon nutmeg
2 1/2 pounds Granny Smith apples, peeled
  and sliced

2 cups flour
1 cup sugar
1 cup packed brown sugar
1/2 cup (1 stick) butter

DIRECTIONS:

Preheat the oven to 350 degrees.

Mix 1/2 cup sugar, cinnamon and nutmeg in a bowl. Add the apples and toss to coat. Spoon into a 9×13-inch baking pan.

Mix the flour, 1 cup sugar and brown sugar in a bowl. Cut in the butter until crumbly. Press 1/2 of the crumb mixture over the apples. Sprinkle with the remaining crumb mixture.

Bake for 25 minutes or until light brown and bubbly. Serve warm with ice cream or whipped cream.

Buttermilk Pie

SERVES 6 TO 8

1 1/2 cups plus 2 tablespoons sugar
3 eggs, beaten
6 tablespoons butter, softened
2 tablespoons flour

1 teaspoon vanilla extract
1/2 cup buttermilk
1 unbaked (9-inch) deep-dish pie shell

DIRECTIONS:

Preheat the oven to 425 degrees.

Combine the sugar, eggs, butter, flour, vanilla and buttermilk in a bowl and mix well. Pour into the pie shell.

Bake for 10 minutes.

Reduce the oven temperature to 300 degrees.

Bake for 1 hour longer.

COOKBOOK COMMITTEE

⚯

Chairman
Carla Sayklay

Co-Chairman, Recipes
Dianne Pasant

Co-Chairman, Project Assistant and Contributor
Laura Hall

Marketing
Lisa Faulkner-Dunne

Mary Bell	Shauna Hartman	Suzann Oliver
Carolyn Bicknell	Pat Heslop	Cheryl Parsons
Susan Caldwell	Teresa Hicks	Janice Renfro
Shelley Chetzron	Karen Hoffman	Kelli Renfro
Mimi Cohen	Linda Holstien	Judi Richards
Suzie Collie	Mary Irons	Kim Roberts
Jean Conner	Tacie Johnsen	Susan L. Rolfe
Stephanie Crowe	Stacy Kovach	Janet Sue Rush
Jeannie Dewar	Cathy Krumholz	Pam Saks
Dana Dill	Jeanne Larranaga	DeLoris Scherschligt
Diane Dodds	Tina Larson	Anne Slatter
Cindy Doyle	Valerie McMahan	Gipsy Smith
Sue Earnest	Sheila Moore	Doris Stigge-Field
Susan Fletcher	Toni Moulter	Donna Thomas
Susan Goldblatt	Vicki Mynhier	B. J. White
Carol Gregston	Mitzi Nevill	Susie Whitehurst
	Patti Nilsson	

RECIPE CONTRIBUTORS

Maggie Adams
Deborah Armstrong
Janet Babcock
Carolyn Bicknell
Joanne Bloom
Debbie Bowen
Linda Bushnell
Susan Caldwell
Shelley Chetzron
Mimi Cohen
Suzie Collie
Delores Cox
Cindy Doyle
Sue Earnest
Shelia Farmer
Susan Fletcher
Dede Furlong
Julia Green
Karen Gregory
Carol Gregston
Laura Hall

Barbara Hammack
Jeanette Harlow
Shauna Hartman
Jean Heinkel
Pat Heslop
Madeline Hickman
Teresa Hicks
Stacie Hobbs
Karen Hoffman
Linda Holstien
Becky Howell
Bertie Howell
Mary Irons
Dede Jackson
Ann Jones
Dale Knopick
Sheila Kostelny
Stacy Kovach
Jeanne Larranaga
Tina Larson

Brooke Leonard
Lavonne Lewis
Betsy Lott
Jill Mansfield
Nancy Marston
Andy McClung
Valerie McMahan
Louise McNett
Debbie Merten
Carol Miller
Mary Moore
Sheila Moore
Vicki Mynhier
Mitzi Nevill
Randi O'Brien
Joan Oxford
Cheryl Parsons
Dianne Pasant
Debbie Penick
Janice Renfro

Kelli Renfro
Deni Richards
Kim Roberts
Susan E. Rolfe
Susan L. Rolfe
Janet Sue Rush
Lynne Rutan
Vicki Sadin
Pam Saks
Carla Sayklay
DeLoris Scherschligt
Judy Searight
Carol Sewell
Anne Slatter
Gipsy Smith
Joanie Smith
Doris Stigge-Field
Bonnie Thomson
Carole Walsh
B. J. White
Susie Whitehurst

RECIPE TESTERS

Janet Babcock
Carolyn Bicknell
Cathy Bourgeois
Susan Caldwell
Pam Carpenter
Shelley Chetzron
Suzie Collie
Dolores Cox
Stephanie Crowe
Jeannie Dewar
Diane Dodds
Cindy Doyle
Sue Earnest
Shelia Farmer
Lisa Faulkner-Dunne
Nan Golden
Julia Green

Karen Gregory
Carol Gregston
Stacy Griffin
Laura Hall
Jeanette Harlow
Shauna Hartman
Jean Heinkel
Teresa Hicks
Stacie Hobbs
Karen Hoffman
Bertie Howell
Mary Irons
Tacie Johnsen
Paul Klocdek
Stacy Kovach
Jeanne Larranaga
Tina Larson

Brooke Leonard
Leah Margerison
Valerie McMahan
Debbie Merten
Sheila Moore
Toni Moulter
Vicki Mynhier
Randi O'Brien
Cheryl Parsons
Dianne Pasant
Debbie Penick
Janice Renfro
Kelli Renfro
Kim Roberts
Susan E. Rolfe
Susan L. Rolfe
Janet Sue Rush

Lynne Rutan
Vicky Sadin
Pam Saks
Carla Sayklay
DeLoris Scherschligt
Judy Searight
Anne Slatter
Gipsy Smith
Doris Stigge-Field
Terry Stine
Lynne Walters
B. J. White
Susie Whitehurst
Susan Wilhoit
Ann Yeargan

UNDERWRITERS

Dianne and Jim Pasant

BRINKER
INTERNATIONAL.

Leah and Rick Margerison
Joan and Terry Oxford

Carla and Richard Sayklay
Tipton Engineering, Inc.
B. J. and Rick White

Karen and Mike Gregory

Nickels and Dimes Incorporated

Maxi-Lift, Inc.

Cheryl and Steve Parsons

Janice and Jack Renfro

Kelli and Mark Renfro

Ronald McDonald House Cooking Team, 2nd Thursday
(Johnnye Allen, Jeannie Dewar, Sue Earnest, Linda Holstien,
Jeanne Larranaga, Sheila Moore, Janice Renfro, Cristina Sellers)

Ronald McDonald House Cooking Team, 4th Wednesday
(Kelly Bennett, Susan Caldwell, Pam Carpenter, Delores Cox,
Mary Irons, Tacie Johnsen, Janet Sue Rush, Gipsy Smith)

Janet Sue Rush and Jerry Mann

Johnnye and Dennis Allen
Janet L. Babcock
The Caldwell Company
Jean and Tom Conner
Dallas Children's Advocacy Center League
Lisa Faulkner-Dunne
Susan Fletcher, Ph.D.
Carol Gregston
Laura and Thomas Hall
Hallmark Homes
Dale Knopick
Sheila and Ron Kostelny
Cindy and John Marshall

Valerie and Lewis McMahan
Mary Ann Paul
Diane and Bill Rhoades
Judi Richards, Ebby Halliday Real Estate, Agent
Joan Robinson and Jeanette Harlow
Susan Rolfe
Pam Saks
Signature Bank
Anne and Lawrence Slatter
Terry Stine
Jackie Thornton
Carole Walsh
Susie Whitehurst

INDEX

TUXEDOS TO TAILGATES

A Celebration of the Seasons

֎֎

Dallas Junior Forum

800 East Campbell Road, Suite 199

Richardson, Texas 75081

972-680-5244

YOUR ORDER	QUANTITY	TOTAL
Tuxedos to Tailgates at $28.95 per book		$
Deep In The Heart at $18.95 per book		$
Postage and handling at $3.50 per book		$
	TOTAL	$

Please make check payable to Dallas Junior Forum Publications.

_____

Name

_____

Street Address

_____

City   State   Zip

_____

Telephone

Proceeds from the sale of *Tuxedos to Tailgates* will support the
charities of Dallas Junior Forum.

Photocopies will be accepted.